Explorations in Awareness

J. SAMUEL BOIS

Explorations
in Awareness

Harper & Row, Publishers
New York, Evanston, and London

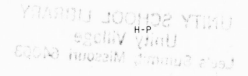

To the memory of
ALFRED KORZYBSKI
whose surveys
in the land of the obvious
have guided these
explorations.

To my wife
CAROLINE HILL BOIS
whose comforting encouragement
made these explorations
possible.

Contents

viii   Contents

Explorations in Awareness

CHAPTER I

On Our Way

✳ Once I was giving a client some training in relaxation. We were just beginning. At this first stage the purpose of the exercises is to make people aware of contraction in a few large muscles. Relaxation comes later.

He was lying flat on his back in a long easy chair with his feet resting on a wide footstool.

First, I pressed against the sole of one foot, and told him to push against my hand as hard as he could, without moving his heel. When you do that, the calf of the leg contracts in such a way that you can't miss it.

"Do you feel any contraction?" I asked him.

"Yes," he said.

"Where?"

"In the calf of this leg."

"Good," I said. "Now, let us do the reverse, and watch well for contraction."

This time I pressed against the top side of his toes, pushing his foot downward and telling him to resist my pressure. This brings about a contraction of the tibial muscle, the long thin muscle that stretches in front of the leg.

He could not feel any contraction there. But I plainly saw his tibial muscle getting hard and shorter.

I touched it lightly with my finger. "Don't you feel any contraction here?" I asked.

He closed his eyes for a moment. "Oh, yes! Of course! Now I feel it. How could I feel it before? I never knew we had a muscle there!"

He could not feel his tibial muscle because he did not know he had one.

It is easier to feel when you know what and where to feel. It is easier to observe when you know what, where, and how to observe.

*   *   *   *   *

The president of a firm had studied a paper I had written to describe the overlapping areas of decision-making in executive work. The whole paper was summarized in a diagram where actions, operations, organization, objectives, and company philosophy were clearly differentiated and put in order.

"You have not told me anything really new," he said, "but you put order in my thinking. It makes it easier for me to observe what is going on. The other day, John Doe, our Works Manager, and Bill Smith, our Controller, were engaged in a discussion in my presence, and I could see them going up and down your diagram, from operations to company philosophy and back, as if they were climbing up and down a ladder."

Again, it is easier to observe what you do or what others

do in your presence, if you have a predetermined scheme to classify your observations. The more realistic the scheme, the more you get out of it.

*   *   *   *   *

The following pages contain nothing that is really new. They describe a few notions that I gathered here and there. Most of them were developed in the course of my professional work with business executives. I found some in books and articles that I read and reread because they helped to clarify my thinking. A few come from conversations with wiser men and women I had the good fortune to meet. All were tried in life situations where I had to decide and do something, in hard times and good times, in many costly blunders and in a few successful ventures.

Years ago, Dr. Brock Chisholm told me something that made an impression on me. "The trouble with most of us social scientists," he said, "is not that we don't know. It is that we don't apply what we know."

I admit that the social sciences are still in their infancy. But they have much more to offer than we realize. By social sciences, I do not mean only psychology, sociology, psychiatry, and the like. I mean every notion that throws light on human behavior. This will bring us into well-trodden areas like religion, into new territories like cybernetics, and into theoretical systems like general semantics.

*   *   *   *   *

Some of my friends who read part of the manuscript for this book, kindly reminded me that I talk a great deal about myself. They say it is bad taste.

Well, there is not much I can do about it. A wise semantician, Elton Carter, summed up the whole problem in a sentence that I must quote: "Did you know that, in all our talking, we are always in a sense talking about ourselves, no matter what else we might believe we are talking about?"[1] The more I ponder over that statement, the more I am convinced that it is plain silly to pretend not to talk about myself. I am not an authority in anything. I have no right to speak in the name of Science, or of anything that sounds well-informed and wise. I can only report my own reactions to what I read, what I saw, what I experienced.

To me, writing a book is like erecting a building. Years ago it was the fashion to set up plaster caryatids that looked strong but supported no weight. Today we streamline the naked pillar that does what it does. Even when we state principles and develop theories, we are not dealing with objective truths that stand out there for everyone to accept or reject. We are summarizing in so many words a mixture of somebody else's views and our own. Science and Tradition, as I see them, are the accumulation of the experiences of people who lived before us. When Freud gave us psychoanalysis, he formulated his experiences with neurotic patients in Vienna; when James wrote his *Principles of Psychology*, he revealed to us his own views of the world of psychology; when Frederick W. Taylor published *The Principles of Scientific Management*, he was describing Taylor's work and hopes.

My own experiences are neither spectacular nor epochmaking. They belong to the world of the average man, who is groping through life, trying to find here and there signposts to better roads. In my explorations I have used various maps. Some proved to be obsolete; some were apparently made from dreams and not from actual surveys; some were

[1] Elton S. Carter, "On the Nature of General Semantics," *General Semantics Bulletin*, 1955, *16* and *17:99*.

hard to decipher but they were well worth the trouble of studying them.

All I can do is to relate my own explorations. Please don't take as authoritative anything that I say. You may decide to put some of my statements to the test of experience. I am confident they will stand it.

CHAPTER II

On Getting Acquainted

✳ They were playing cricket in
Westmount Park. It was a sunny Saturday afternoon in
October, and some two hundred people had stopped in their
stroll to watch the game. I stopped too, sat on one of the
benches, and tried to understand what was going on. I
counted the players: there were eleven on each side, all
dressed in white, some with leggings, some without. The
pitcher is called a bowler: he throws the ball with his arm
kept straight in an awkward way. The batsman does not hit
the ball with the vigorous swing of a baseball player; he
seems just to block it with his flat, wide stick. Both the bowler
and the batsman stand near what they call a wicket, which
is nothing but a diminutive fence made of three narrow
posts joined by a crosspiece at the top.

The movements of the players are most unpredictable.

They never run fast. They seem to watch for something that never happens. They show a subdued excitement that never breaks out in the open.

All this is very confusing to me. Cricket is a mystery. I still wonder what those Englishmen see in it. Compared to baseball, it does not make sense.

Why is it that cricket does not make sense to me? In fact, there are many other games that do not make sense to me. Chess, for example. I remember that two-hour train trip from Ottawa to Montreal when two fellow psychologists were absorbed in a never-ending game that kept half a dozen onlookers panting with a mysterious excitement. To me, it was an exhibition of childish behavior on the part of a group of otherwise sensible confrères. Today, I see myself fascinated by a chess game. Why? Because I have learned the function of the various pieces and I see their movements as parts of a meaningful strategy.

I have a similar experience when I read a book. It is like cricket or chess. If I know what each playing unit is supposed to do, how it is related to other units, how the action of one changes the pattern of the whole moving group, it makes sense to me, and I enjoy the game.

Reading a book, an article, or even a paragraph, is like a game. It makes sense to me if I know what the key terms are all about, how they relate to one another, how they combine into patterns that change in meaningful succession. Reading a book is a matter of getting acquainted with its key terms: what they are, where they come from, what they are expected to do in the context, how they interact with one another, how they combine in meaningful patterns.

Bertrand Russell formulated this idea long ago in what he calls the *Principle of Acquaintance:* "Every proposition which we can understand must be composed wholly of constituents with which we are acquainted."

Wittgenstein and the Vienna group gave another principle which tells us how to get acquainted with the constituents of a statement. Theirs is called the *Principle of Verifiability:* "A proposition is significant if it is logically possible that it should be verified by one reporting an experience."

So, we have three steps that are pretty definite: 1) spotting the key terms of a statement, 2) getting acquainted with them, and 3) making that acquaintance meaningful by relating the terms to personal experiences.

Among the books that have influenced my thinking, there is one to which I shall refer very often in the following pages. You may have heard of it; you may have attempted to read it; you may have read it many times. The book is *Science and Sanity*, by Alfred Korzybski.[1]

You may have found it difficult and confusing at the start. So did I, for the first six or seven years. I kept reading it and pondering over its very knotty statements because I found it a stimulating challenge every time I opened it, and also because each little discovery that I made here and there encouraged me to carry on.

As time went on, I discovered a way of making more discoveries with less groping. Little by little the structure of Korzybski's monumental work came into the clear, with some parts artfully completed, some half worked out, some merely sketched and left for us to finish according to his overall plan.

One of my most spectacular discoveries was in finding a passage in which Korzybski gives us a clear-cut directive as to how to work through his book. Why in the world didn't I

[1] Alfred Korzybski, *Science and Sanity: An Introduction to Non-Aristotelian Systems and General Semantics*, 3rd ed., International Non-Aristotelian Library Publishing Company, 1948. By permission of the Alfred Korzybski Estate.

pay attention to these few lines when I read the book in the first place? You probably know why. My case is the classic one of a reader who finds in a book what he is prepared to find, and misses many things that are put well within his range of vision. The same thing may happen to you as you read these pages. I may say things that are so obvious that you will pass them over as unimportant, or I may use far-fetched analogies and illustrations that you will consider irrelevant and confusing. This difficulty is inherent in all communications, particularly when we are set upon the groping, pioneering, and blundering task of revising and correcting our "common sense" outlook on things.

Well, what was that simple directive that I missed for many years? Here it is: "Readers who are interested in this work will facilitate their task if they *make themselves familiar* with these new terms and *use them habitually*. This work will then appear *simple*, and often *self-evident*."[2]

Here, by *new* terms, I understand not only the words coined by Korzybski himself to describe notions that are not found elsewhere, such as *multiordinality* or *semantic reaction*. I refer to other words that he took from common usage and to which he gave a sharper or different meaning—for example, *abstraction*. I am speaking also of many words which, because of his mathematical and scientific background, had for him a meaning that did not coincide with what they meant to me— for instance, the words *system, function, structure*, and the like.

Prior to "discovering" the passage quoted above, I had made a few experiments in teaching General Semantics; these had shown that certain difficult passages became simple and self-evident when I took time to explain with concrete examples what the key words of these passages were used to represent. Let me tell you of one such case:

[2] *Ibid.*, p. 64. Italics mine.

The organism is not an algebraic sum, a *linear* function of its elements, but always *more* than that. It is seemingly little realized, at present, that this simple and innocent-looking statement involves a full structural revision of our language, because that language, of great pre-scientific antiquity, is *elementalistic*, and so singularly inadequate to express *non-elementalistic* notions. Such a point of view involves profound structural, methodological, and semantic changes, vaguely anticipated, but never formulated in a definite theory. The problems of structure, "more", and "non-additivity" are very important and impossible to analyse in the old way.[3]

I felt that there were three key words in this passage:
1. "elements" (or the adjective *elementalistic*)
2. "structure"
3. "*more*," as different from the additive "*plus*."

Other unusual terms such as "linear," "algebraic sum," "non-additivity," and the like, would become clear as we went on.

I started with a simple demonstration derived from Gestalt psychology, first tracing twelve vertical straight lines of equal length, like this:

Each line can be considered as a part, or an *element* of the total picture. They are lined up like a row of soldiers at attention, and this is what we mean by *linear* presentation. As we number them, from left to right, we *add* them up, and the total picture is a *whole* made of *additive elements*.

The elements may be grouped in fours, if we want, and the

[3] *Ibid.*

total picture will remain *linear*, or unidimensional in its over-all arrangement. Thus:

Now, if we place these elements differently, we may have a picture that represents surfaces instead of lines, passing from discrete parts to a whole of two dimensions. Thus:

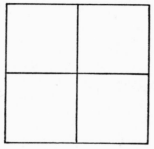

Here we have *no more* lines than before, but the total picture cannot be described by saying that it is made of twelve lines. The arrangement (the structure) is of a different order. The *whole* picture is *more* than a row of lines; it is an *area*. The *elements* are the same as before; the *whole* is different.

The next jump is more spectacular. If we arrange the twelve lines as follows, we have a cube:

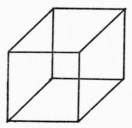

This picture says *much more* than the original row of lines, and in this case it is evident that the word "more" does not mean "plus." It means a different, more complex, order of structure. Something has been *added*, without *increasing* the *number* of elements, but by *arranging* (*structuring*) them differently.

After giving this demonstration, I asked the students to read the quoted passage again, and in all cases they found it more simple and more meaningful than it had appeared at first. Read it again yourself, and you will see what I mean.

After this enlightening experience, and many similar ones which I cannot relate in full, I kept wondering: "Why in the world didn't Korzybski state somewhere that his work would become crystal clear to those who take the trouble to study his key words, become familiar with them, and use them consistently?"

I had the proper question in my mind, worded disparagingly in reference to the author as you see, but it was there anyway. One good day, when I read for the *n*th time the passage, "Readers who are interested in this work will facilitate their task if they make themselves familiar with these new terms and use them habitually," it suddenly dawned on me that my "discovery" had been well-indicated on the map that our dear old friend draws for us. My question should have been: "Why in the world didn't I pay attention to Korzybski's statement that his key words are the key to his system?"

If these key terms are studied one by one, it may help, but it is not sufficient. We are so *elementalistic* in our thinking that we may miss the structure while trying to grasp the elements one by one. These key terms have to be studied in their relation with one another; they throw light upon one another.

Instead of defining them as in a dictionary, I have found it more practical to work gradually towards a better understanding of them by means of analogies, demonstrations, and experiments. Finally, I have made use of diagrams, and I recommend them strongly, because I have found by experience that visualization[4] is a powerful tool to communicate complex notions.

I must add that in the following pages I do not limit myself to the Korzybskian key words that I choose to use. I introduce some of my own.

[4] *Ibid.*, pp. 452-468.

CHAPTER III

Language as a Tool

✳ There are many things you can do with a hammer: you may drive nails and pull them, split a board, break stones, bang someone on the head, and so forth. But there are things that you cannot do with a hammer: you cannot saw a piece of wood, drive a screw, or bore a hole.

A tool has a function, a range of uses. The limits of that range are not always very sharp; a skillful worker may achieve wonders with the most primitive tools. But there is a point where he has to stop because the tool is totally inadequate to do what has to be done. With a stethoscope and a thermometer a good physician can diagnose many ailments, but he will need a microscope to examine a sample of tissue that he suspects of being cancerous.

The tool is not independent of the tool-user, and the tool-user is not independent of his tool. Taken together, they form an operating unit that works as a whole. Tools can be considered as extensions of man's sense organs, and of his arms, hands, and legs. The automobile gives us the seven-league boots of fairy tales, the airplane gives us wings, the hydraulic press gives us the muscular strength of a Titan.

What of our brain? Have we any tools that have increased its power, its speed, and efficiency? Yes, we have. A child in the elementary grades of school can now perform long multiplications and divisions that were considered as the exclusive achievements of experts in the Middle Ages. The tool that he is using is the positional notation of numbers, or the device of giving a number ten times its original value when we write it in the first column to the left, one hundred times its value when we write it in the second column, and so forth. This was a great invention which came from India through Arab scholars. History shows that it was resisted very strongly for generations, just as the first labor-saving devices were not welcomed by manual laborers in the early days of machinery. To appreciate the difference between this mathematical tool and those that were used before, divide CVIII by IX, using exclusively the Roman numeral notation, and see how long it will take you to get the answer.

Like physical tools, the brain tools have their limitations. They are very useful within a certain range of operation, but they cannot cope with problems outside that range. For instance, the metric system, based on the decimal notation, passes much more easily from volume to weight than does the cumbersome English system of feet and pounds. But if you try to express *exactly* in decimals the one-third of a meter, you cannot. To profit by the advantages of the metric system, you must forego the measurements that are inconsistent with it. No tool can do everything; no system is an all-purpose system. If your brain adopts a tool, it increases its capacity and limits it at the same time. We choose our tools according to what we have to do; we have to become better acquainted with our brain tools and change them freely when we have to.

We are coming now to a most important notion. Unless we agree about it, we are bound to misunderstand each other in the following pages. So, please take time to ponder over the statement emphasized a few lines further down. You may find it obvious, baffling, mysterious, exaggerated, or what not—I don't know. To me, it is a key statement. If you don't accept it, please do not go beyond it,—or proceed at your own risk. Here it is:

OUR EVERYDAY LANGUAGE CAN BE VIEWED AS A BRAIN TOOL.

Language as a tool. What does this mean in the light of what has been said before? It means this:

1. Language is the tool we use to do most of our thinking. In other words, thinking could be described as *talking to ourselves.*

2. The better the tool, the better the job. A rich and flexible language makes thinking rich and flexible.

3. The language and the thinker (the tool and the tool-user) form a working unit, in which each element helps and limits the activities of the other.

4. Language is organized into a system by virtue of its rules of syntax, and it throws out of our thinking unit—that is, out of our functioning brain—all statements that are inconsistent with its system, just as the metric system forces us to ignore the exact third of a meter.

5. If we become aware of the limitations of our language, we may recognize what limitations it imposes upon our brain.

6. By pushing outward the limitations of our language (by improving the tool range and the functioning of the tool) we may increase the capacity of the human brain, as the mathematicians did when they removed the shackles of the Roman numerals and introduced the positional notation.

Are we going to compare languages, say French and English, Russian and German, Nootka and Cree, and decide which is the "best" thinking tool? No. I am not a linguist, and I don't think anyone has both the competence and the authority to promote such a change.

Are we going to insist on those "increase-your-vocabulary" exercises and tests that appear in the *Reader's Digest* and similar publications? No. A larger and more precise vocabulary is surely a good thing, but while it increases the *elements* of our language, it does not affect its *structure;* it does not bring it to a higher dimension.

Are we to advocate a new language, either simplified from a current one, like Basic English, or derived from a whole family of related idioms, like Esperanto, Volapük, or Interlingua? Not at all.

Are we going to become purists, people who dabble in etymology, Greek roots, and word history, for the purpose of restoring the *pure, original* meaning of words? Nothing is further from our purpose.

These questions, and similar ones, are all going in directions where countless pathways have been trodden down by pioneers and their eager followers. If you expect a new version of any of these schemes, or a combination of some or all of them, you will be disappointed.

Our explorations will take us in other directions and into other dimensions. Our starting point is that language can be viewed as a tool that combines with our brain to form one thinking unit. You have noticed it when you attempted to learn French, Spanish, or any other language. For a while you kept *thinking in English* while clothing your thoughts with the terms of the new language. Eventually, the new thinking tool became "homogenized" with your brain, and you discovered that you could think either in English or in the new language. Translation meant "re-thinking" the experience or the stream of thoughts in a different language.

The tool and the tool-user form a complex unit. We may separate them "mentally," but in practice they work as a whole.

CHAPTER IV

More About Tools

✳ Let us put some order in our think-
ing about tools. Since the tool and the tool-user form an
operating unit, we may, by studying the tool and its functioning, get a clearer idea of how they increase and limit the
power of the tool-user.

The automobile is a transportation tool: it increases our
speed from four miles an hour to sixty or better. It gives us
greater endurance: we may keep on going for hours at a time.
Three years ago it gave me the strength to carry my family
and a load of baggage from Montreal to San Francisco and
back. It made me a tireless giant, crossing the plains and
jumping over the Rockies in steps of hundreds of miles,
enjoying the scenery as I went along.

But the automobile has its limitations as well. It has to
follow the road; it cannot roam the fields, cannot take to the
trails that would bring us to certain scenic spots. It needs gas

and oil; it cannot live on the natural resources of the land as it goes along. It has a complex mechanism that requires attending to. Otherwise, it may become a pile of junk lying helpless, miles from nowhere. Standing by this pile, the automobilist (the user of this particular tool) is just as helpless as the machine on which he was depending to get him where he wanted to go.

The airplane is another transportation tool. It is faster than the automobile, independent of road conditions, capable of cruising over land and sea. It made possible the airlift in Berlin when the Russians closed the roads; it brings travelers from Vancouver to Amsterdam by flying over the icy vastness of the North Pole. But its limitations are sharp and stringent; they affect the tool-user (the flyer) to such a point that his own survival often depends on the performance of his machine. The tool and the tool-user are very closely identified with each other. If the flyer attempts to do what is beyond the range of his plane—for instance if a jet flyer attempts to land on too short a strip—both he and his machine run the risk of complete destruction.

A tool has limits, and the limits of the tool control the tool-user's freedom to act as he pleases. You may turn a sharp corner when you walk; in an automobile you must reduce your speed according to the bend of the curve; in a locomotive you have to follow the track; in a speeding plane you may have to trace an arc of many miles to change your direction.

If we accept the notion that language is a thinking tool, we must face the problems of language limitations. What we say of language applies equally to any other form of representation: mathematical symbols, geometrical figures, diagrams, pictures, and the like. No tool is an all-purpose tool. No language, no symbol system can express everything in every way desired. Thinking, because it is carried out by means of a language tool or a symbol tool, is necessarily limited to the range of the tool itself. Korzybski had his own cryptic way of saying all this in a simple statement: "The map does not represent all the territory." The *map*, in his terminology, meant the picture you draw in your own mind, or the picture you convey to others by means of words, gestures, and drawings. The *territory* means *what is actually going on*. It means that "chunk" of reality, spread in time and/or space, you are dealing with—for instance, the sunset you want to describe, the vacation you spent at the seashore, the feelings that went through you when you got that engagement ring, and things like that.

As you read this, you may find that my comparison of language and man-made tools is a bit far-fetched; you may feel that I stretch a point beyond reason. Please don't give up at this moment. We are now struggling to reëxamine one of those common-sense notions that we habitually take for granted. In fact, we are trying to disentangle a whole skein of common-sense notions that are tied together in knots, such notions as the following:

1. Language and thought are two different things.

2. When I do not find the "correct" expression, I can look for a better one.

3. If I define all my terms carefully, I can convey exactly what I mean.

4. By increasing my vocabulary, I can improve my language without limits.

5. An "intellectual" tool is not like a machine, and the mind is not limited in its activities as the body is limited in its movements.

6. This tool approach is too materialistic to help us understand things of the spirit.

We could continue in this vein for pages and pages. Many such vigorous objections occurred to me when I encountered the notion of language as a tool for the first time. I wrote down a few of them; you probably could write many more.

Well, let us not be disturbed by these difficulties. My experience has been that the best way to handle them is to shove them aside for the time being. If we push the tool analogy a bit further, it may throw more light upon certain aspects of our "mental" and "emotional" life than we ever thought possible. If the analogy of the tool proves fruitless, we shall throw it aside as being itself a very poor tool. Before taking a decision, let us give the analogy a good try.

Speaking of languages, we must admit that very few of us can think and speak fluently in languages that are strikingly different one from the other. English, French, German, and a host of other tongues belong to the family of Indo-European languages. They are cousins, as it were, and they have much in common. To come back to the tool analogy, I would say that they are all machines of the same general type: some of French make, some of English make, some of German make. The parts are not strictly interchangeable, as any of us knows who has tried to tighten an English bolt with a French nut. But, on the whole, they perform similar functions, and the limits of one, if any, are pretty close to the limits of the other. If one of them is inadequate for certain purposes, it is likely that they all suffer from the same shortcomings.

Yet, if we look closely, we may detect differences that are significant. Let me tell you of a personal experience that will illustrate what I mean.

French is my mother tongue. I learned English at school, but it was not until I was seventeen or eighteen that I set myself earnestly to the task of learning to speak and think in English. It was an unpleasant task, I must say. I had no great desire for learning a language which, at the time, I considered inferior to mine, and poor in logic and clarity. But I *had* to learn it to make a comfortable living in Canada, where English was then, even more than today, the language of business.

Once we were given the original French text of the national anthem "O Canada" to translate into English. When I came to the following lines:

> Près du fleuve géant
> Le Canadien grandit en espérant,

I wanted to have the correct English word for "fleuve." I had heard people speak of "The St. Lawrence *River*," but I was sure that the word "river" could not be the exact translation. "River" means "rivière," and anyone who has sense knows that a "rivière" and a "fleuve" are two entirely different things. So I thought then.

I looked in my dictionary. To my great surprise, "fleuve" was translated by "river." This could not be right, evidently, and my dictionary was too small. I looked into a larger one. Same thing: only one English word, "river," to translate both "rivière" and "fleuve." What a discovery! I had a vague suspicion that English was a very poor language compared to French, but I had never thought that the difference could be that great. Even in such simple tasks as naming the natural objects, English was short of words. What will it be when I try to render in English the subtle nuances of our French authors?

I could not believe my eyes. It seemed all so absurd, so impossible! I could not be the first person to hit upon such an obvious flaw in the vocabulary of the English. Hundreds of English scholars must have noticed the lack of a proper word to name "fleuves." They must have coined one, or used the French term itself. What could I find in their best dictionaries, on their maps, in their geographies?

My search was fruitless. By sheer stupidity, or by some unconscious collective blockage that I could not explain, English-speaking people all over the world had ignored for ages part of the objective world around us; they had navigated "fleuves," not suspecting that they were not sailing rivers, but something entirely different. No wonder they could not appreciate our pride in the mighty St. Lawrence, on the shores of which we French Canadians are growing with hopes overflowing.

A little later I had to translate English into French. The word "giggle" was in the sentence. From the context I knew fairly well what it meant, but I checked in my dictionary to make sure of the exact translation. The French term was "ricaner." You see, for every English word, we have at least one French word—clear, precise, picturesque.

Further down came the word "titter." I knew it referred to something fairly close to "giggle," but I wanted to perceive the difference more clearly by using the exact French equivalent. To my disappointment, there was none. "Titter" and "giggle" had one translation in French: "ricaner." Oh, well! Why should one make such fine distinctions when describing the behavior of some silly little girl?

In another context there was the word "chuckle." It referred to a big fat man whom I could almost see and hear chuckling with amusement. How do we say that exactly in French? Well, well! I could hardly believe it: "ricaner" is the only word we have. The score was turning against us, and I was disturbed.

My feeling of French superiority received a crushing blow when I eventually looked for the French translation of "to sneer." Little did I expect that once again I would find the ubiquitous "ricaner" in a context that I knew had nothing in common with "titter," "giggle," or even "chuckle."

The moral of the story is that I don't see the same things, I don't observe the same events when I change my English for my French thinking tool. Changing my language changes me as an observer. It changes my world at the same time. I cannot dissociate my senses and my brain from the tool I am using. In English I break the jigsaw puzzle of the world around me into pieces that do not fit exactly with the pieces I obtain when I break it into French pieces. The frames of reference are different; the pieces are not interchangeable in all cases.

This can be illustrated by a simple diagram. Let me represent the goings-on by a circle. In French I see them like this:

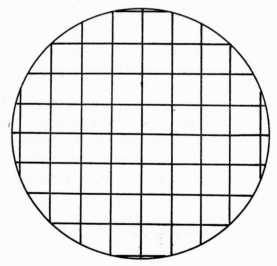

In English I see them like this:

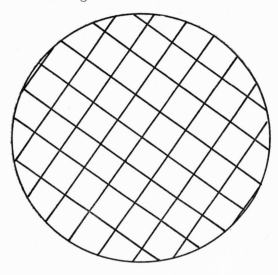

Can I superimpose one pattern on the other? No. Can I superimpose one French piece to fit exactly its English counterpart? No.

These diagrams are too simple to give us a full account of the differences between French and English thinking. Our language gives us more than a flat, two-dimensional picture of the world. It gives us rules on how to combine and move these pieces in time to represent the flow of events. This is where the use of tenses increases our differences.

In English we use the present to refer to some action which in French is definitely located in the future. For instance, we say: "When I *have finished* reading this chapter, I shall pass to the next one." In French, this makes no sense at all. We have to use the future to convey the same meaning: "Quand *j'aurai fini* ce chapitre, je passerai au suivant." In other words, the English present stretches into the future and overlaps with the French future tense. The breakdown of the time dimension is different in the two languages.

There are other differences as well. The modes of thinking introduce shades of meaning, thinking vectors that cannot be reduced to a common measure. What of the French subjunctive, of the English "shall" and "will," of the gerund that makes a noun of a verb? How can I say in plain French: "We live in a world of goings-on?"

In the light of this discussion, I understand better what Miss M. Kendig means when she says of Korzybski that he "had nothing to say . . . before he came to America, made English *his* language, formulated his functional definition of man in this book."[1]

[1] Alfred Korzybski, *Manhood of Humanity*, 2nd ed., International Non-Aristotelian Library Publishing Company, 1950, p. xvii.

CHAPTER V

Statements, Theories, and Systems

✳ So far, we have stressed the differences among our Indo-European languages. We know that certain terms are not translatable because their original meaning is so deeply imbedded in the language from which they emerged. Think of the "Weltanshauung" of the Germans, of the "élan vital" of Bergson, of the "time-binding" energy of Korzybski. Each of these terms was created with a tool that has left on them a lasting imprint, and they cannot be used to full advantage unless they are handled with the same tool.

Is there a common framework to our Indo-European languages? Yes, there is. The purpose of the following pages is to uncover this common framework, to examine it, and to become aware of what it does to our thinking. Ours is a difficult task. I approach it with trepidation. I hope you are approaching it with an open mind.

Whenever we make a statement, we imply a theory. For instance, if you say: "I am 40 years old," you imply that:

1. you consider the calendar year as a unit of time.
2. you take this unit of time as a practical measure of your life.

If you say, "This leaf is green," you imply, among a number of other things, that:

1. there are colors in this world.
2. this color is different from others.
3. this color is visible to the naked eye.

If you say, "John hates his father," you imply that:

1. there is a feeling, an attitude in John which can be differentiated.
2. this attitude is opposed to love and respect.
3. this attitude is likely to create misunderstandings and conflicts between John and his father.

You could make a different statement about this same behavior of John and say: "John has an Oedipus complex." This would imply the Freudian theory of the unconscious, of complexes, of the sexual origin of complexes, and similar ideas.

If you are an Adlerian, you may describe the situation in terms of dominance-submission, implying an unconscious as a Freudian would, but seeing the will-to-power as the active agent within John.

A statement can be seen as contained within a theory, explicit or implicit. A scientific statement is easily recognized as part of an explicit theory; common-sense statements are not so easily linked to formal premises or postulates. Nevertheless, we can see that no statement stands all by itself; no statement is ever made outside a theoretical framework

A particular theory may be contained in a more general

theory: for instance, the Freudian and the Adlerian interpretations of behavior are both particular theories that fit within the general theory of psychoanalysis. They are different in some respects, but they have in common the notions of the unconscious, the complexes, and the repressions.

Finally, we may look at a great many theories, particular or general, and picture them as parts, aspects, or elements of a *system*. Thus, the various chapters of physics we studied in high school deal with different aspects of the physical world: mechanics, acoustics, optics, and thermodynamics, but they are all within the Newtonian system. In a less formal manner, the Newtonian system is the background of our common-sense thinking about the universe. A simple statement such as "this steak weighs seven pounds," involves the theory of gravitation, which is within the Newtonian system. Our languages, by their very structure and organization, grammar, inflections, and parts of speech, are expressions of theories imbedded in our cultures. All Indo-European languages have for common background a system inherited from our Greco-Latin forebears. This system, as pervasive in the social sciences as the Newtonian in the physical sciences, is called by Korzybski the Aristotelian system.

When we use the word "system" here, we are dealing with one of those key terms about which we must agree if we want to understand each other. This word is used often in scientific literature. Ludwig von Bertalanffy, for instance, writes about his General System Theory, and about "closed" and "open" systems. The same word is used in common parlance as well; we speak of filing systems, transportation systems, metric system, nervous system, and system of government. None of these meanings, scientific or popular, applies here. By "system," in these pages, we mean *a body of theories that involves a common method of thinking about the world and ourselves*. It refers

more specifically to that method of thinking itself, exem-
plified in theories that may either agree or clash with one another. The Freudian and the Adlerian theories do not agree
on all points, but they both fall within the general theory of
psychoanalysis. Similarly, democratic and communistic
doctrines clash on many fronts, but they both fall within a
common system of thinking, in the sense we use the word
"system" here.

In Korzybski's writings[1] you will recognize the three
notions—statements, theories, and systems—that I am dis-
cussing here. There is a slight difference in terminology,
however, which I must clarify.

By the word "statement," I refer to what Keyser and
Korzybski call "propositions" and "propositional functions."
In simple, more or less exact language, we may say that a
proposition is *what I say about an event.* A propositional function
what I can say about an event. It is the mold, the ready-made
structure that serves to cast a proposition. The proposition
(or statement), "this leaf is green," is cast in the mold "leaves
are colored."

By the word "theories," I refer to *doctrines* and *doctrinal
functions.* We can describe a doctrine as *what I say about a
selected cluster of events that I consider related to one another.* The
doctrinal function refers to the set of molds or templates that
can be used to relate to one another the events of the selected
cluster. It is a verbal structure intended to correspond to the
empirical structure of events. In the case of the green leaf, this
would mean theories of color, vision, and the like. When a
selected cluster of events is considered as part of a larger
cluster, for instance, when color is studied as part of optics, or
vision as part of psychology, we have particular doctrines
within more comprehensive doctrines, or sciences within

[1] Korzybski, *Science and Sanity*, pp. 133–150.

more general sciences. Some people use the word "systems" to describe these broad doctrines or sciences. I don't.

When it comes to "systems" and "system-functions," I choose to limit these terms to what Korzybski means. By "system," I refer to *how I structure my sayings about events, cluster of events, or clusters of clusters of events*. "System-function" becomes the structured matrix, imposed upon my thinking-feeling processes by the assumptions buried deep in the culture in which I grew, or explicitly stated in a set of postulates that I accept consciously. To continue with the example of the green leaf, our language imposes upon us a subject-predicate way of thinking, a substance-and-qualities view of the world that puts me in a particular relationship with the cosmos. As long as I evaluate the goings-on within this system-function, I remain cloistered within a world of things and actions, of substances and qualities, described with nouns, pronouns, verbs, adjectives, and adverbs. This system-function is the framework common to Indo-European languages. To view this framework from outside, we have to study languages of a very different structure, as did Benjamin Whorf and others.

It is relatively easy to change and/or correct a statement. It is more difficult to change a doctrine for a different one. When it comes to passing from one system to another, the task is Herculean. It is tantamount to a revolution in our way of life.

History shows that the discovery of isolated, though interesting, facts has had less influence on the progress of science than the discovery of *new system-functions* which produce *new* linguistic *structures and new methods*. In our own lifetime, some of the most revolutionary of those advances in structural adjustment and method **have** been accomplished. The work of Einstein, the revision of **mathematical** foundations, the new quantum mechanics, colloidal

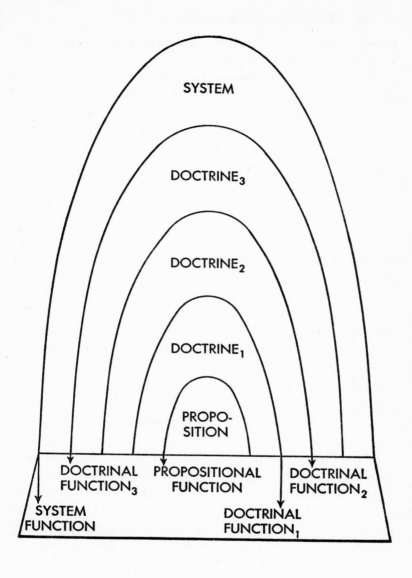

science, and advances in psychiatry, are perhaps structurally and semantically the most important. There seems no escape from admitting that no modern man can be really intelligent in 1933 if he knows nothing about these structural scientific revolutions. It is true that, because these advances are so recent, they are still presented in very technical terms; their system-functions have not been formulated, and so the deeper structural epistemological and semantic simple aspects have not been worked out. These aspects are of enormous human importance. But they must be represented without such an abundance of dry technicalities, which are only a means, and not an end, in search for structure.[2]

We may now sum up this chapter in the accompanying simple diagram made of overlapping curves resting on a baseline. Within the small inside curve (propositional function) we have the propositions or statements of facts. They lie within the next larger curve (doctrinal function) which includes all the key assertions of this doctrine. This, in turn, may be part of a more comprehensive doctrine or science (doctrine$_2$), which may also be within a still broader doctrine (doctrine$_3$). Eventually we come to the largest curve that contains all the smaller ones. It represents the system-function, and its area covers the system within which all doctrines (sciences) and propositions are locked.

When Korzybski gave as a subtitle to his huge volume, "An Introduction to Non-Aristotelian *Systems* . . . ," he meant (at least this is my interpretation): "An attempt to break out of the prison that our language has built around our statements and our prevalent doctrines, and to reach for the freedom to create, test, and revise an indefinite series of systems more and more adequate to our self-propelled growth in the knowledge and mastery of the world and ourselves."

[2] *Ibid.*, p. 148.

CHAPTER VI

A Program of Guided Awareness

✳ To the question, "What is General Semantics?" there is no simple answer. Yet, I consider the question a reasonable one. I take it as meaning something like this: "Where do you put this thing you call General Semantics in the diagram you outlined? Is it a theory (a science)? Is it a system?"

To visualize an answer to this question we can draw a three-dimensional diagram that shows statements, theories, and systems on a series of planes that grow in size as mankind advances from its primitive stages to the present day. The semantician makes an attempt to stand outside this array of planes, and he takes a critical look at man progressing through the ages. As the semantician observes and formulates his observations, he makes statements. These statements are related to one another in a science that he structures as he goes along. In developing this new science, he holds fast to the postulates of a new system, different from the closed system of his language and culture, and consistent with the advances that have been made in the physical sciences.

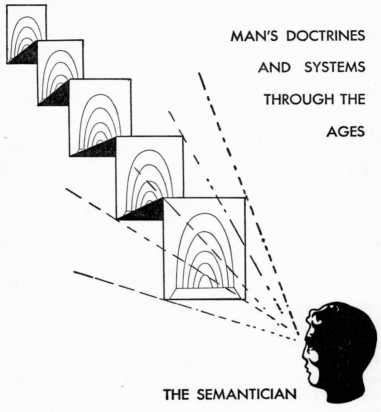

MAN'S DOCTRINES

AND SYSTEMS

THROUGH THE

AGES

THE SEMANTICIAN

As a consequence, General Semantics involves a revision of "common-sense" statements, a rearrangement of the present theories and sciences of human behavior, a restructuring of the framework of our Indo-European languages and of the methods of thinking-feeling that are articulated with them. It can be viewed as a program of guided awareness, of educated consciousness of what is going on in the world and within ourselves.

If I call General Semantics a science in the ordinary sense of the word, like psychology, biology, or physics, I lock it within the old framework drawn on the nearest plane of the three-dimensional diagram. By doing so I disregard its distinctive characteristic. Yet, I must admit that it includes new "scientific" formulations, such as multiordinality, semantic reactions, and the extensional definition of man.

I may call it a system, as Korzybski does,[1] provided it is understood that this system is still in its early stages of development and requires considerable work to become formulated from explicit postulates to theorems, corollaries, and applications.

We may also describe General Semantics as an empirical science, based on unprejudiced observation and directing us towards experimentation in every field of human endeavor, from the speculations of the creative scientist to the day-to-day activities of the man-in-the-street, down to the aberrations of the neurotic and the psychotic.

This attempt of man to look at himself as he goes along—living, thinking, feeling, moving, growing, and shrinking in a world of which he is a part—is not an altogether new enterprise. It has been given different names depending on the particular elements of this activity that were emphasized. It became ontology or metaphysics, theology or religion, ethics, epistemology, humanism, and what not. Korzybski appears at a loss when he tries, at different times and in different contexts, to choose a word that could be taken as a descriptive label of his life's undertaking. He speaks of "humanology,"

[1] Korzybski, *Science and Sanity*, pp. 92–94.

of a "science of man," of "human engineering," and of a "general theory of evaluation." How he came to introduce the term, "*General* Semantics," for "the *modus operandi* of this first non-Aristotelian system,"[2] remains one of those fortuitous events to which we may give too much importance. This is a case where the Shakespearian question, "What's in a name?" surely applies. Personally, I have grown to view the whole thing as *a program of guided awareness*. I do not suggest this phrase as the best definition of Korzybski's contribution to man's development, but it gives me a general orientation that will become more and more evident as we go along.

I came to this orientation by a zigzagging, circuitous way. There were many years during which I rebelled against Korzybski's insistence on "consciousness of abstracting" as the main aim of his work. To me, abstracting was merely an "intellectual" affair, and I blamed the old man for being a cut-and-dried epistemologist, exclusively concerned with the brain, and bothering very little with emotions, feelings, and moral values. On the first page of his book, he lists the names of fifty-five men whose works he says have greatly influenced his inquiry, and he dedicates his system to them. As far as I could see, the common feature of all these men was that they were *thinkers*. Some of them could be classified as moralists, but not all. My inference was that Korzybski was placing himself, and his system, in the parade of thinkers who come through the ages holding aloft mottoes and slogans dealing with intellectual pursuits. I could see his epistemology different from that of Aristotle or Plato, but, in my own elementalistic way, I saw epistemology as only one aspect of human life, and a very limited one at that. When I saw on the letterhead of the Institute of General Semantics that it was

[2] Korzybski, *Science and Sanity*, 1st ed., p. viii.

"for Linguistic Epistemologic Scientific Research and Education," I became more convinced than ever that the whole enterprise was one of abstruse theories and philosophical hair-splitting. When I studied Chapter XXIX, "On Non-Aristotelian Training,"[3] I saw the Structural Differential as a marvelous device to develop consciousness of order in our thinking activities, yet one devoid of any provision for the control of feelings and the appreciation of human values.

At the time, I did not suspect that I was suffering from the schizophrenia that we consider "normal" in our culture. My outlook on human behavior was split in two: on one side there were intelligence and thinking; on the other side there were values and feeling.

When I go over the chain of events that brought me to such an impasse, it seems to me that the importance of key terms becomes more and more evident. The two terms that misled me were "abstraction" and "epistemology." They belonged to my acquired vocabulary, and I took it for granted that in the Korzybskian context they meant exactly what they meant elsewhere. After all, abstraction is abstraction, and epistemology is epistemology! To abstraction, as I knew it, I added the new notion of orders of abstraction, which corresponded quite closely to the distinction between the specific and the generic. I was pleased with myself: Korzybski had not taught me anything that was really new; he had simply clarified and sharpened my own thinking.

Epistemology? Of course, I knew what it meant! It is the science of our knowing activities, it deals with doubt, certainty, opinions, and facts. There again we are on the brain side of human functioning. I agreed that in our days of relativity and of the uncertainty principle, a new episte-

[3] *Ibid.*, pp. 469–490.

mology was needed, and I welcomed the Korzybskian formulations.

I was missing something, though. Deep within myself, I felt there was a whole world of feelings, emotions, and values, of motivation and purposes, that this new system did not penetrate. In fact, I did not expect an epistemological system ever to invade this world. The brain and the heart were separated by an iron curtain built within me by the system-function and the doctrines I had absorbed in my cultural environment. I did not know the curtain could be removed; I thought I was born that way. And I missed every passage in *Science and Sanity* that said differently.

It was not until I "discovered" another key term in General Semantics that I saw through the iron curtain. This term is "semantic reaction." It is fully analyzed by Korzybski in Section A of Chapter II,[4] and given as *fundamental* in the new system. It is said to cover all reactions that were formerly covered by the *elementalistic* terms "emotions" and "intellect."

It may be a good idea to begin our explorations in awareness by taking a good look at these semantic reactions.

4 *Ibid.*, pp. 19–34.

CHAPTER VII

On Semantic Reactions

✳ Let us represent the many activities of man by drawing four ellipses that overlap to some extent. Three of these ellipses cover activities that are within the range of common observation. We shall label them C, B, and A. The fourth one deals with activities that are revealed by scientific instruments and techniques; they remain somewhat mysterious to the casual observer. We shall label it X.

In the top ellipse (C), I include all activities that are termed *thinking*. As I am writing this, I think; you also think as you read. In thinking I include "ideas," language, symbols, writing, reading, talking, listening, figuring out problems, planning, and like activities. A financial statement, a newspaper, a sales graph, a letter, a telegram, are things that we use to think and to communicate our thoughts.

In the next ellipse (B), I include activities that come under the term *feeling*. We can recognize the differences between thinking and feeling. Feeling refers to pleasure, joy, anger, fear, desires, purposes, moods, regrets, wishes, worries, disappointment, enthusiasm, curiosity, and boredom. There is

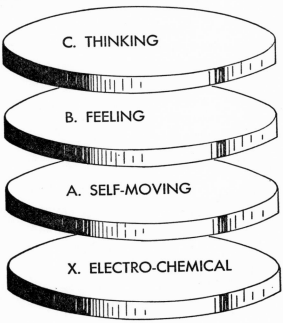

Four Aspects of Man's Activities

feeling connected with a family gathering at Christmas, a date with a girl, a raise in salary, a sudden illness of a loved one, a handshake of appreciation, a kiss, a joke, the discovery of a fire in the basement, stage fright, the expectation of an interesting trip, or the planning of a new house.

Ellipse (A) includes what I choose to call the *self-moving* activities. This covers the autonomous functioning of the organs and the voluntary movements of our bodies. The heart pumps, the lungs expand and contract, the whole body grows. A man works with his hands, he walks, speaks, shouts, sings, cries, laughs, eats, drinks, marches in a parade, dances, drives a car, grows pale, or is flushed.

Ellipse (X) covers the *electro-chemical* activities that have been discovered and measured by scientists. This represents the field of electrocardiograms, electroencephalograms, and electromyograms; of anesthetics, insulin, vitamins, hormones; of the lie-detector, and of electroshocks.

These various activities overlap and they interact; when something happens in one section, something happens in all

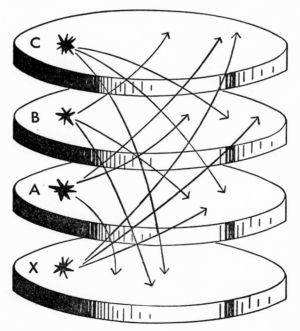

Interaction of Man's Activities

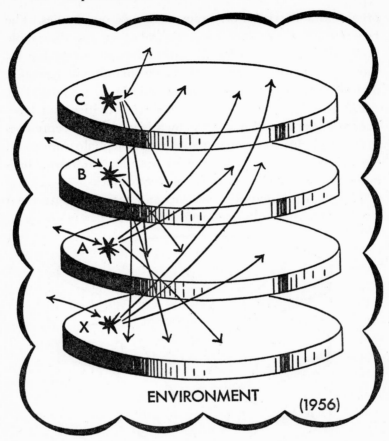

**Organism (C.B.A.X.) as a Whole
Interacting with Environment
at a Date**

others. When you think hard, you become tense; when you are emotionally upset, your thinking goes awry; when you are given an anesthetic, you stop thinking and moving. You bring about feelings of friendship by inviting people to lunch or to cocktails; Hitler made his people march in parades to indoctrinate them and direct their feelings; worries often cause ulcers; insulin-shocks clear up the confused thinking of some patients. This can be illustrated by arrows that criss-cross from one ellipse to the others. Man is an organism that works as a whole.

Finally, we realize that we cannot divorce this organism from its environment of both time *and* space. A man may be born with a native ability comparable to that of Einstein, but if he grows up among Australian aborigines, he has little chance of improving the theory of relativity; a genius born in the fourth century before Christ could not produce Mendelyeev's table of chemical elements. An adult has been molded by his earlier life, by his cultural milieu, his work, and his experience. Moreover, man modifies his environment and changes it as he goes along. Generations of men have transformed the Nieuw Amsterdam of the Dutch settlers into the New York City of today. This complex environment is shown here by surrounding the four ellipses with a freely drawn boundary. A three-dimensional drawing conveys the idea of both the organism's and the environment's extension in time.

This brings us to a description of man which could replace the standard definition: "Man is a rational animal." We may say: "Man can be described as a thinking, feeling, self-moving, electrochemical organism in continuous interaction with a space-time environment."

This organism reacts to whatever goes on within or outside itself. He reacts to events distributed on the time line. He may react at this moment to something that went on years ago, that is going on now, or that he feels may happen tomorrow or in the distant future. His reactions reach out in space. By

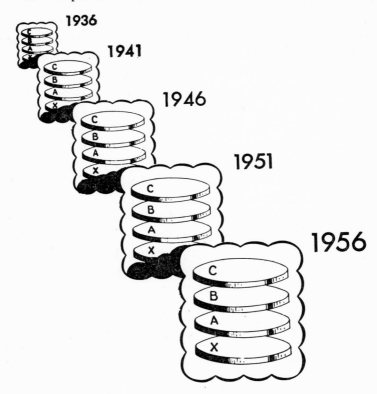

Organism-Environment in Space-Time

instrumental means (radio, television, or written messages), he reacts to and influences events that are distant. As he reacts, he interprets and evaluates each single happening against his individual experience and anticipation. His reactions are *semantic* reactions. He lives in a world of "happenings-meanings."

This can be illustrated by the following diagram. Let us represent three persons by as many diagrams as we described in the preceding paragraphs. The first one represents a physician; the second, his patient; the third, a research technician who keeps records in a hospital. Let us label them S (Specialist), P (Patient), and T (Technician).

Above these diagrams we write a statement from the pa-

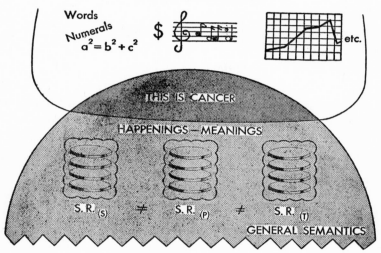

Semantic Reactions Differentiated from Meanings of Symbols

thologist. It contains a very simple message: "THIS IS CANCER." The word "cancer" is clear enough. We may assume that all three persons agree as to what it means. But do they react to it in the same manner? Evidently not. The condition that the word stands for does not mean the same thing to all three. It is easy to realize that their semantic reactions are different at all levels of activity (C, B, A, X). What the physician does involves thinking for the most part; the patient is in the throes of depressive feelings; the technician simply moves his pencil to make a tally on a statistical chart.

The dictionary meanings of words and the semantic reactions to words are two different things. The first belong to the "world of symbols"; the second to the "world of happenings." These two worlds overlap when a word is taken into the stream of life and assumes a unique meaning for the person hearing it or using it at a particular moment under particular circumstances.

Semantics deals with the world of symbols and their meanings. *General* Semantics deals with the world of human reactions to symbols and happenings as evaluated by a total organism at the moment of contact. It deals with "happenings-meanings."

There are many conclusions that can be drawn from what has been described so far. Here are a few:

1. No two persons react to any word or symbol in exactly the same manner. We can agree on an average meaning of a word or statement. But what the word or statement means to the other fellow at a certain moment is never exactly what it means to me at the corresponding moment. The four areas of activity (C, B, A, X), and the space-time environment of two individuals never coincide.

2. Our own semantic reactions never repeat themselves in exactly the same manner. The dynamic balance of the C, B, A, and X areas varies constantly and the environment changes also. A word or a statement cannot mean to me today what it meant last month under different circumstances. If I try to be rigorously "consistent," I may fail to adjust to change.

3. There is no reaction that is purely "physical" or purely

"psychological." The organism reacts as a whole. If I hurt your feelings, I hurt you in all areas. If I oppose your views, I am fighting you at all levels.

4. Whatever happens that is behaviorally significant involves more than the verbal level. The words and symbols we think with, pronounce, hear, or write, are part of the happening. They often play an important role in the event. But their effective meanings depend on the total (space-time) human experience in which they are inserted.

5. The important thing in human relations is not to know what words mean, or to be clever at putting them together in a neat and logical manner. A superior person is not necessarily an expert in words. He is a person who has developed an awareness of what is going on within himself and within his environment.

6. Bodily processes of the other person—his postures, tensions, flushings, and the like—convey messages that may be more potent than words. Shakespeare calls this "a kind of excellent dumb discourse" (*The Tempest*, Act III).

7. When we try to solve a problem by ourselves, we are not juggling with disembodied "ideas" that are either true or false, right or wrong. We are tossed about by our own semantic reactions that are alive, sensitive, dynamic, and responsive to space-time pressures, of which we are not always conscious. Problem-solving may be a laborious process that wears us out if we don't know how to manage it at all four levels described above.

8. When two or more persons engage in the study of a practical or theoretical issue, they are not simply fitting together the pieces of a jigsaw puzzle, each of which has a predetermined place that will be recognized by all once it is found. They are huddling together in a fenced-in area a

crowd of semantic reactions, each of which comes in with its acquired momentum and direction. These reactions push one another, clash or join momentarily, rearrange themselves in a variety of dynamic patterns, line up for an accepted purpose, stop the struggle in a compromise, or leave the scene hurt and mangled by a fight where no quarter was given nor received. Unless we are aware of what is going on in such an encounter, we cannot deal adequately with the situation.

CHAPTER VIII

An Important Distinction

✳ In our search for awareness, we are now coming to a most important distinction. It may seem so obvious at first that you will wonder why I stress it so much. But please remember that our job is precisely to pierce through the hard shell of the obvious, to break it open, as it were, and to discover what lies within it.

In the preceding chapter we spoke of the *world of words* and the *world of happenings*. They overlap in our semantic reactions, as we saw in the "cancer" diagram, and our personal world becomes a *world of happenings-meanings*, different from the world of anyone else.

When we speak of the world of happenings, we refer to what is going on outside ourselves and within ourselves, whether we observe it or not, whether we *can* observe it or not. As I write this in my study, facing a window that looks out on the trees and the lawn, I hear the masons chipping stones to build my neighbor's house, the carpenters sawing boards and hammering nails, the pump that starts and stops when the faucets are opened and closed in the house, the planes that fly overhead, the birds that chirp in the trees, the leaves that rustle in the wind, the faint scratching of the pencil on the paper, the voices of my wife and children in the kitchen, my own blowing out of the smoke I have inhaled from my cigarette. I see my desk, my papers and my books, the vine creeping outside the window, the cedars, the spruces, and the elms in the background of the landscape, the yellow patches on the lawn scorched by the sun, the piles of lumber and stones on the neighbor's property, the men who move around and gesticulate, the clouds that float in the air, the calendar on the wall, the Danish vase beside it, the lines of script that cover more and more of the page as I go on. Within me there is a mixture of feelings: "How much of this should I describe to convey what I mean? Who will have the patience to follow such a personal story? How can I say as much without so many details? Shall I finish this chapter today? Is all this worth the trouble?"

I could continue indefinitely, realizing as I proceed that when you see the words in print you will experience very little of what is going on here this August morning. A colored motion picture and some recordings would give you more; but how can I give you the feel of the hot humid day, of the reactions and sensations that are going on within me?

So far, we have paid attention to what is going on at the level of our common observation, at the *macroscopic* level, as the scientists would say. What is going on at the level that the microscope and other scientific instruments can reveal is beyond imagination: the cells in the leaves of the trees, the electrical discharges that go through my brain and muscles, the chemical exchanges in every tree branch, in every blade of grass, the ultraviolet and the infrared rays in the light. If I pass from the *microscopic* level of happenings revealed directly by instruments, to the *submicroscopic* level of atomic science, the whole scene becomes a dance of swirling electrons and energy waves in which I almost lose my identity.

Even when I speak of the whole scene I have attempted to describe, I must remember that I am dealing with a mere fragment of what is going on in this small village, in the Montreal area, in the country, in the world at large. I limit this fragment to an arbitrary measure of time—this August morning. And what is going on now, or went on before, that bears a more or less direct relation to this little group of events? God only knows.

Are words, pictures, or any other forms of representation capable of conveying all that? Obviously not. The verbal level (and by this I mean whatever I can say to myself or to you) has no common measure with what Korzybski calls the "objective" level. What is going on and what I say or can say are of two different orders of existence. What I say *is not* what is going on. What I say draws your and my attention to a few limited aspects of what is going on. By itself and of itself the objective level is *unspeakable*. It is *silent* in the sense that it does not interpret itself until a conscious individual emerges and gives it a meaning.

The meanings will depend very much on what aspect we emphasize, on the manner in which we speak about it. For instance, I can say of this morning, "It is hot and humid," or "This is a good day to keep away from the city," or "We are already halfway through the month and behind in our schedule," or "The builders next door are making too much noise."

The language we use draws attention to certain aspects of what is going on, and the manner in which it forces us to think and speak gives a particular interpretation to the events of our life. On the one hand you have the dictionary, grammar, and the rules of logic; on the other, you have the flow of events of which you are a part. When you choose certain words and arrange them in a statement, you give a pattern to your interpretation of the world, and this *interpreted* world becomes for you the only world that you deal with at the moment. The unspeakable realm, when combined with the spoken word, becomes the semantic world in which we live. Of the two components of this semantic world, the verbal element is the one which the inventors and lawgivers of our language have structured for us. Because of that structure, we grow, live, think, feel, and behave according to rules we seldom question, unless we engage in such explorations as we are carrying out now.

The main trouble is that we often believe that what *is going on* is what *we say is going on*. It works fairly well in simple cases, but it often creates unnecessary problems. The hidden implications of what we say cause us to look for things that are not there. Poincaré gives an example which has become classical: in the days when very few chemical elements were known, scientists were trying to isolate the element *heat*. Why did they look for heat as an element comparable to sulphur, oxygen, or mercury? Because it had a name that belonged grammatically (and therefore logically) to the same class as that of elements, the class of nouns or substantives. By implication, substantives referred to substances (or elements), and consequently, the scientists were looking for the substance heat, or *phlogiston*. But it was not there. Back of that substantive was a process, not a permanent element like sulphur, oxygen, or mercury. What the language said and implied *was not* what was going on.

There is a similar problem with the word *memory*. Memory is a noun, and a noun is a name for something. Implicitly we assume that we have more or less of that something, that it is working well or poorly, that it can be lost, destroyed, or restored. So, people complain that they are "losing their memory," or that they have a "weak memory." Yet, they may at the same time tell you that they cannot forget this or that unpleasant incident. Their memory is strong and persistent, and yet it is weak and poor. What a problem! What a contradiction! The problem is in the word that is used and in the *thingness* it implies. If we replace it by a word that refers to a process, to an activity, and speak of "re-membering," the whole problem can be tackled differently. Instead of asking, "Why is my memory sometimes poor, sometimes good?," we may ask ourselves, "How is it that I remember this, and do not remember that?"

This may become tragic at times. I remember a client who came to me years ago. He was selling insurance and his income depended on his ability to talk prospects into buying policies. Unfortunately, he had developed a strange psychosomatic trouble: his salivary glands would cease functioning while he was speaking, and his mouth dried up to a point where he could hardly continue. The dryness of his mouth was unpleasant and made him feel that his breath smelled bad, turning people away from him. I was helping him to correct these reactions, when a well-meaning friend met him one day and made this remark: "Well, Jack, you look better. Did you get rid of that obsession?"

The word "obsession" hit my client like a thunderbolt. An obsession, for him, was *something*, lodged somewhere in his brain and devouring his nervous system. He believed that what he thought was *really there*. It took him weeks to get rid of the monster that words had created in his semantic world.

In our semantic world, we all have roads, road blocks, mountains, valleys, bridges, cities, transportation systems, communication networks, wild beasts, fairies, leprechauns, wise men, shamans, and rulers. Most of them were there when we were born—created, installed, or let loose by past generations. We learned to accept them as part of the picture. We take them for granted, and we don't question their presence. The world in which we live is the world that our cultural group has made and organized according to its common-sense statements, its doctrines, doctrine-functions, systems and system-functions. We assume that the world *is what we have learned to say it is.*

This can be visualized by making a few changes and additions on the diagram already used to demonstrate systems. We cover with hatches the left half of this diagram, and we write the words "proposition" (statements), "doctrines," and "system" in their respective places on the right-hand side of the diagram. The left half represents the *silent, unspeakable level, the world of events or happenings, the mysterious region of what is going on.* The right half represents the *verbal level,* the *world of words and other symbols,* the clear region of *what we say about happenings.* This right half is the area of language, logic, mathematics, of deductive reasoning and consistent "thinking." The left half is the area which we assume has a structure, about which we like to form theories.

Every statement, doctrine, and system has some explicit or implicit assumptions or beliefs as to what *is*. These beliefs, guided for the most part by what we have learned to say about the world and ourselves, are consistent with the struc-

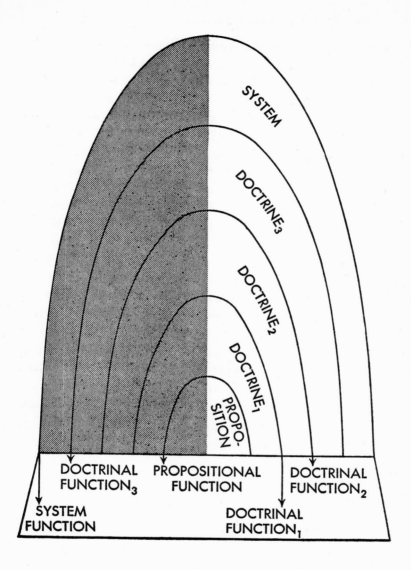

SYSTEM

DOCTRINE₃

DOCTRINE₂

DOCTRINE₁

PROPO-
SITION

DOCTRINAL
FUNCTION₃

PROPOSITIONAL
FUNCTION

DOCTRINAL
FUNCTION₂

SYSTEM
FUNCTION

DOCTRINAL
FUNCTION₁

ture of the language and symbol systems that we use. If our symbol system is three-dimensional, as in Euclidean geometry, the structure of the world is assumed to be three-dimensional; if our logic is multi-valued, as in modern science, the structure of the world is assumed to be multi-dimensional.

We have a tendency to believe in the cosmic validity of generally accepted statements. We have a tendency to believe that the structure of the world is similar to the structure of our common-sense logic. We make predictions and we have expectations from the right half of the diagram; we expect events to happen on the left side according to what we have figured out. When they do, we conclude that we have found a *law of nature;* when they don't, we restructure our theories and try again if we behave as scientists, or we become frustrated and rebel against Providence if we don't.

This clear-cut distinction between the silent (objective) level and the verbal (logical) levels is itself a man-made theory, I know. But it has proved to be helpful, and we shall come back to it again. By using it as a thinking tool, we shall pass from the stage of implicit, and often blind, beliefs, to an awareness and an acceptance of degrees of probability.

CHAPTER IX

A World Made to Our Image

✳ The right half of the diagram (page 57) is the area of symbols; the left half, the area of happenings. Korzybski compares the right half to a map, to a sketch that we make of the left half. The left half he compares to a territory, which the map is intended to represent.

On a map we use conventional signs to represent the features of the territory. Take an ordinary road map, for instance, and you see that superhighways are indicated by a double solid line in most cases; standard highways are shown by one solid line; secondary highways may be of a different color; roads under construction appear as broken lines. The size of towns and cities is translated into dots, circles, and colored areas of different design. Mountains, airfields, railway lines, streams and rivers have their own symbols. A military map will show more detail. A geological map will bring out different features. A weather map will have to be changed every day to follow the movements of air masses, clouds, and winds. In all cases, the practical value of a map depends on how well it guides us in the territory for the purpose at hand. Its conventional signs must distinguish features of the territory that are sufficiently unlike others to make a difference for the traveler.

Does our language work in all cases with the adequacy of a good map? Unfortunately not. Too often we fail to agree on what a key term is intended to mean in a particular context, and we get lost. We have done our best to avoid such a confusion in earlier pages by describing as precisely as possible what feature of the territory—what particular activity, notion, or behavioral mechanism—we referred to when we use the words "element," "structure," "doctrine," "system," and others.

We now come to one very common word of our everyday vocabulary, which is so simple that we do not suspect its complexity. This most dangerous word is a form of the verb "to be," the third person singular indicative: "is."

Before studying the term "is," let us start with another word, the common verb *to have*, which, in my experience, has helped to introduce the message I want to transmit.

If you look in the dictionary for the word *have*, you will find a whole string of meanings, from *to hold* or *possess*, to such things as *to experience, to be obliged to, to enjoy*, and the like. I agree with you that the context will tell you what special meaning you must give it in a particular statement. For instance, you know that "I have a mosquito on my neck" does not describe a happening that is exactly identical with "I have a pain in my right side." In the first case, you may kill the mosquito or chase it away; in the second, you may want a surgeon to take out your appendix.

In some cases the parallelism may be more evident, and yet the behavioral meanings may be miles apart. "I have one hundred dollars in my wallet," and "I have one hundred thousand dollars in mining stock" do not stand in the strict proportion of one to a thousand times one. The second "have" involves risks, possibilities, taxes, and preoccupations that are almost completely absent from the first.

The meanings of common words are seldom as sharp as the meanings of the conventional signs on a map. We could, and I suppose we should, be aware of the differences in meaning that make a difference in our life, but we do not always act that way. To chase the pain or to kill it with a sedative is not the same as to chase the mosquito or to kill it with your hand. When your investment shrinks to one-half its original size, it is not the same as when you spend half of the money in your wallet.

In our semantic reactions, these various shades of meaning often overlap or become blurred. Our thinking becomes oversimplified, and we take it for granted that an overall, general meaning is good enough for practical purposes.

This brings me to the tricky word "is." It is used in four ways:

1. As an auxiliary: "He *is* working." This involves no difficulty, and we need not worry about it.

2. As meaning predication: "This leaf *is* green." You had better watch this one. It introduces into our language map a structure that does not exist in the world of happenings.

3. As meaning identity: "This dog *is* an animal." This one is a treacherous indicator that leads us nowhere.

4. As meaning existence: "The lamp *is* on the desk." This always involves a belief that a definite feature of the territory corresponds exactly to what the language map says.

The trouble is that we pass easily from meaning (2) and (3) to meaning (4). We take for granted that what we say corresponds to what exists; that the manner in which we describe a happening corresponds to the manner in which it happens. When we say, "This leaf is green," we assume (and believe implicitly) that a) there *is* a leaf clearly cut out of the process continuum; b) there *is* greenness in that leaf, and c) the leaf and the greenness *are* two separate things. Whenever we say, "It is so and so," we imply that "it *is*." Our statements appear to have a cosmic validity. In fact, we boast of their being "objective." So much for meaning (2), which lies at the very core of our subject-predicate language, of our map of the world in terms of substances and qualities.

The jump from meaning (3) to meaning (4) is just as easy and just as misleading. The statement, "This dog is an animal," implies that a) there *is* a dog clearly cut out of the process continuum; b) that "animality" *is* out there, in the world of happenings, and c) that this dog and animality exist out there, fused and blended in a composite whole. Whatever we say it *is* has *to be*, otherwise, how could we say that *it is so?* What a play on this verb *to be* in a short sentence! After the manner of Gertrude Stein we might say, "This leaf is green, this leaf is, the green is, this leaf is is is, the green is is is" or, "This dog is an animal, this dog is, an animal is, this dog is is is, an animal is is is." As the "is" keeps reverberating like an echo within the walls of our inner self, we take it for a message from outside, revealing to us the existence of a world unwittingly made to our image.

Do I deny an "objective" reality? No, not at all. But I am leery of the validity of our interpretation of this "objective" reality. I am (I exist); the world is (the world exists). This I can't deny. But the world is not what I say it is. The verbal level is not commensurate with the silent level. It *often* gives me a distorted picture of the silent level. It *never* gives me a complete picture of the silent level.

CHAPTER X

Are Words Only Words?

✳ The *world of symbols* is one of those key terms that may be misleading. "Words are words," you may say. "I cannot see why you attach so much importance to words as such. We are not always talking; we think, we love, we hate, we have preferences, likes, dislikes, habits, customs, social standards, personal ambitions and purposes; we have a culture, a civilization, an individual style of life. To bring all of these to a mere matter of words seems to simplify human life arbitrarily. You build a straw man and burn it at the stake, but man as a living being remains untouched and very much alive."

For many years I felt the way you do. I am in sympathy with your difficulties because they were mine. Let me describe to you how I moved from where you are to where I stand now. You don't have to move the way I did, but my experience may give you some inkling as to where my road was blocked and how I removed the blocks or went around them.

I was not ready to accept the idea that *thinking is mostly talking to myself*. I felt I could think without words; often I had the impression that my thinking was richer than the words I could find to express it. Words were like clothes with which to dress my thoughts, but I knew that my naked thoughts were different from the clothes they wore.

I have not changed much on this point. I don't find it necessary to change much. Far from it—I think that I see this better than before. I describe this phenomenon differently, and by describing it differently, I understand it better. What I used to call my "thoughts," richer than words, I now call "first-order experiences," unspeakable, belonging to an order of existence that is different from the order of existence of words, "mental categories," "ideas," "mental constructs," "concepts," and such. These first-order experiences belong to the left-hand side of the diagram (page 57), to the *silent* level, to the world of happenings. I am conscious of them, but the minute I start describing them to myself or to others, I am also conscious that I am not "holding" them in their living totality. I cannot help but betray this first-order experience when I attempt to translate it into words, "ideas," "concepts." I am aware that *it* (the first order experience) *is not what I say it is*.

Korzybski would illustrate this point by a simple experiment that often appeared childish to his listeners. "Pinch a finger," he would direct us to do, "and see if you can convey by means of words this first-order experience (what you do and what you feel) to the person next to you." To me, it was a revelation. I *knew* what I did, I *was aware* of what was happening, but I had never realized that *being aware* of a happening is not the same as describing it to myself or to others. I did not have to describe it to myself to be aware of it, but I could not match my description with my awareness. Strangely enough, I realized also that a more explicit description sharpened my awareness. Awareness and description are different from each other, and they interact upon each other in a mysterious way. For the time being, let us note well that "awareness" refers to first-order experiences and that we can differentiate it from "thinking," or second-order experience.

This sharp distinction between "being aware" and "thinking" was for me a considerable advance. I was under the impression that my words were like clothing to dress up my thoughts. Today, I see my first-order experiences as live models, my "thoughts" as mannikins made of plastic that look more or less like the models, and my words (or symbols) as the material out of which I can build the mannikins. Depending on the material I use, on the measurements I take, and on the skill I possess, the world of mannikins is an almost exact replica of the world of models. But it is not the world of the live models. The trouble is that we often behave as Pygmalion, falling in love with the mannikins we have constructed. Here we play God, breathing the breath of life into the clay we have molded. We may even go farther in our delusion: we make gods and goddesses of our own creations. We call them "general principles," embodying Absolute Truth which every one must revere.

In the light of this distinction, I began to see our culture in a different light. I saw that I was born into a world of mannikins which I had not learned to differentiate from living experiences. Some of these mannikins were articulated—

their legs, their arms, and their bodies could be moved like those of the statues I saw Mexicans use in their religious plays. They were clothed in royal garments or in rags, depending on what the directors of the play wanted them to represent. They even spoke, gave orders, warnings, suggestions. They ruled my world like so many Frankensteins set into motion by invisible powers: "*Science* declares . . . , *Religion* demands . . . , *Logic* prescribes . . . , *Psychology* has discovered that. . . ." The most ubiquitous of them was Common Sense, a hydra-headed monster, often nicknamed "They," "People," or "Human Nature." "What will *They* think? What will *They* say? *People* don't act that way. *Human Nature* does not change. *People* will not give up war."

The directors of that mad play were dead, many of them, but the play was still going on. Geometry was gesticulating in three dimensions as Euclid had set it going; Logic was asserting identity, as Aristotle had prescribed; Religion threatened; Science insisted on counting; Physics ignored the speed of light. A self-anointed priesthood had withdrawn itself from the world of ongoings to keep these idols intact in an artificial world of absolutes, occasionally replacing the old gadgets with more efficient robots, or clothing in resplendent robes the ragamuffins of yesteryears. The *Hundred Great Books* would shackle us instead of *Tradition; National Security* would take the place of *Inquisition;* the *Law of the Jungle* would become the *Survival of the Fittest;* and *Propaganda* would be transformed into *Adult Education* or *Public Relations. National Sovereignty* is the Moloch to whom we now would sacrifice thousands of victims in the scorching fire of the atomic bomb. Happenings have to conform to what we have learned to say and persist in saying.

The world of words is also a world of "values." When we

give a name to a happening, we determine *where it belongs* in an up-and-down, left-and-right assortment of desirable or undesirable thingumbobs to which we react according to the place we have given them. Give a dog a bad name, and it will live up to it; give a man a high-sounding title, and he will feel bigger. I know from personal experience that it feels different to be called a *Canadian citizen* instead of a *British subject*. Advertising experts exploited this human mechanism when they translated, for instance, "Cheap Clothes for Fat Old Women" into "Limited-Income Clothes for Dignified Maturity." When the Russians speak of communistic countries as "peace-loving nations," we don't like it. In fact, we always imply value when we look for the *proper* expression, the term that fits our semantic reactions (page 47).

It is all that, and much more that is consistent with it, that I mean by this *world of words* represented in the right half of the diagram (page 57). You may call it by other names, if you prefer. Some authors speak of "semantic environment," and I think it is a good term. For me, however, the word "environment" kept the whole thing outside of myself. It took me some years to realize that this environment was not like a geographical location, of which I can be independent to some extent. I now see it as something that penetrates me like the air I breathe. It goes deep within my system, ruling the vital exchanges between my first-order experiences and my innermost "thoughts."

Some will speak of "culture" or "cultural milieu." This evokes in me a keener appreciation of the value aspect of this world. I had a tendency to associate *culture* with the groups to which I belong—the national group, the social group, the professional group, or the religious group. I do not disregard this aspect, far from it. But to pin down the whole thing to something concrete, to something I can handle, as it were, I prefer thinking in terms of words which I can change, arrange differently, experiment with. For instance, I know from repeated experience that by introducing a new term in the everyday vocabulary of a group of executives, we can change the "climate" of the group and bring about a shift in their attitudes.

Words are not only words. Symbols are not merely signs that we can manipulate with detachment. I prefer viewing them as tools, indispensable and extremely useful, part and parcel of our human equipment for living as human beings. With them we shape our semantic reactions into a world of our own making.

CHAPTER XI

Meet Smith_n

✳ Against this world of words I see what I call the "world of happenings," the world of events, the objective world of what is going on within me, around me; way out through space and reaching to the most distant stars in all directions; way back in time to what I picture as a beginning of some kind, and far into an indefinite future. Scientists speak of "events" or "point events," of "cyclical ongoings," of "quanta of action," interacting ceaselessly according to some complicated laws of multidimensional order. The proverbial man-in-the-street contents himself with the report of his unaided senses, and he sees a world of objects, organisms, places, and historical sequences to which he gives names according to the language he has learned and to the purpose he has in mind. We already have seen that the "chunk" of ongoings that we call "rivers" in English is split into two separate categories in French, one called "rivières" and one called "fleuves." Any happening may be described with different terms in one language, depending on what aspect you want to emphasize. If you whistle, you may say that you utter a "sound." Hold the outer surface of your hand near your mouth as you whistle, you will say then that you produce a "draft" of air. What *is* it? A sound or a draft of air? It depends on which feature you want to talk about.

Happenings, or events, may be of different dimensions in space and in time. When I behold this world of ongoings, I can cut out from the background a tiny detail like the speck of dust that dances in the sunlight over my desk; I can see in a single sweep the blue spruce on the lawn; from an airplane, I can survey the whole city as we come down to the airport. My span of attention can narrow down to a very short moment in time or it can encompass a long period of history. I can deal with this minute or this second; I can review at one glance the week I spent at Star Island; I can lump together my years in college, my whole life, or a period of history.

When I lump things together in this fashion, I may miss the trees because of the forest. When I look at each tree separately, I may miss the forest as a whole. All depends on what I want to take into account. If I could find a way of doing both at the same time, it would be quite an achievement. It might give me a fresh view of the world of happenings, a richer awareness of what is going on. It would add a new dimension to my outlook in the space-time dynamic fullness.

Mathematicians have devised a means of doing just that. They have created symbols representing at the same time both the particular and the general, the individual event and the class to which it belongs, the uniqueness of the one and the common features of the many. They do it by attaching to a name that refers to the whole class a number (or subscript) that pinpoints each individual within the class. For instance, they will write $house_1$, $house_2$, $house_3$, . . . to $house_n$ ("n" meaning *any* number) to indicate to what they refer when they speak of houses in general, without losing sight of the uniqueness of each single house that exists, has existed, or will exist.

Korzybski often repeated that mathematics is a language, and he insisted that this language has tremendous possibilities to stimulate and enrich our thinking. At first he annoyed me no end when he was hammering this message at me. I saw mathematics as a weird juggling of cabalistic signs that had nothing in common with genuine human values. This attitude of mine persisted until, one good day, I started meditating on what he calls his "extensional definition of man," and drew from this meditation a wealth of insights. I shall try to give you some of them.

By "extensional definition of man," Korzybski meant a mathematical representation of the whole of humankind, in time and in space, from the first *homo sapiens* to the baby born this very moment. He summed it up in a simple expression, derived from the mathematical language that meant so much to him. The expression is $Smith_n$.

Smith stands for a proper name, like yours or mine. It reminds us that no individual answers to the common name "Man," but has a distinctive one of his own, be it Robert, Pierre, Ivan, Chou, Juan, or Xenophon. The number attached to each name is unique for each individual, as if you witnessed an almost endless parade of all the Smiths who lived and are now living on our planet—man, woman, or child—different one from the other as to age, culture, occupation, place of abode, mental capacity, health, feelings, and ambitions. This helps us visualize the human race in space-time, moving about all over the earth through prehistoric times and recorded history; from the primitive in his cave to the city dweller in his penthouse; from the demented in mental hospitals to the scientist in places of higher learning; from the beggar who stretches out his hand for a pittance to the millionaire who signs checks of astronomical size; from the newborn who yells his first cry to the dying who breathes his last; from the underworld character to the nun in her cloister; from the leper to the winner of a beauty contest; from the soldier returning home in victory to the crippled victim of the Hiroshima blast. See them appearing and disappearing, milling about along the paths of history, all over the continents. Their crafts and their habits are changing as time goes on; their way of life differs from one place to another. The Smiths today live differently from the Smiths prior to the Industrial Revolution; these in turn lived differently from the Smiths of the Middle Ages, and so on, back to the Smiths who hailed as geniuses the inventor of the wheel and the discoverer of fire-making.

In this space-time multitude, I see groups and subgroups appearing and disappearing: families, tribes, associations, nations—growing at different rates, blending, and separating again. Looking at this motley crowd on the march, I observe certain types of activities that I single out as distinct clusters, conscious all the while that these clusters overlap and blend to a great extent. I see these activities as dynamic bundles of similar experiences, knowledges, behaviors, traditions, practices, and institutions that I classify under different labels. I call them religions, sciences, arts, mathematics, war, industry, human relations, and so forth.

I view Religion as the space-time cluster of $Smith_n$'s semantic reactions related to cosmic experience. It covers the animism of the primitive, the pilgrimages, the shrines, the rituals of all creeds, the sacred books and the theologies, the reverence of the scientist of today. It blends with Metaphysics, explicit or implicit.

I view Science as the space-time cluster of $Smith_n$'s semantic reactions related to predictive experience and behavior. It stands in close relationship to Mathematics, or the conscious manipulation of numbers and relations.

I view Art as the space-time cluster of $Smith_n$'s semantic reactions related to visual, tactile, auditory, and rhythmic experiences. When I think of it, I remember the saying of the poet, "A thing of beauty is a joy forever."

I view Human Relations as the space-time cluster of $Smith_n$'s semantic reactions related to interpersonal and intergroup contacts. It has something to do with private and public morals, family life, organizations and institutions as such.

If you feel like it, carry on your own meditation, and describe to yourself how you can view war, industry, politics, government, or anything you want to study, in terms of the semantic reactions of $Smith_n$. You will probably come, as I did, to accept these general terms as mere indicators of what you are trying to locate in the vast moving panorama of human activities. You may become less and less concerned with such questions as these: "Is this art or not? Is this real science or not? Is this genuine religion?" You may see no contradiction between $Smith_1$, who talks of the Last Supper as a religious painting; $Smith_2$, who evaluates it as a work of art; and $Smith_3$, who admires it as a geometrical design. You may understand better a woman who sat next to me at a lecture given by Hayakawa on General Semantics and Modern Art. He had shown us colored slides of Paul Klee's works. During the question period, she asked him what was so artistic in that Paul Klee. Hayakawa answered patiently, and explained how one can become used to such paintings and eventually see their beauty. She listened with equal, or nearly equal patience, and thanked him for his answer. Then she turned to me and said under her breath: "He may say what he likes, but this is *not art*. It's just horrible!"

What is art? What is science? What is religion? To me, it boils down to whatever activities of Smithₙ we agree to include under each one of these labels.

When I describe the world of happenings, I have found it a good practice to use Smithₙ as a unit of discourse. It is a label that corresponds to something definite, to men, women, and children in the flesh. It means more to me than the abstract word "man," which is a name for a thought, and not for a first-order experience (page 65).

CHAPTER XII

The Worlds of Smith$_n$

✳ Each one of these Smiths lived (or is living at this moment) in a world of his own, different from the world of anyone else. In a sense, there were, there are, and there will be as many worlds as there were, there are, and there will be Smiths on this planet of ours. Each one of us is the center of his own individual world, the only world that he knows, the world that grew with him and that will disappear with him.

If the above statements appear strange to you, please do not dismiss them as mere figures of speech. What I am trying to do now is to bring you with me on an exploration beyond the borders of the obvious. It may turn out to be an interesting voyage. The map of the voyage is entitled, "The Worlds in Which We Live" (page 77), and you may refer to it as we go on.

76

This map is made of four concentric circles lying on a white background. Each circle is designed to represent an aspect of the world experienced by Smith$_n$ in the course of his

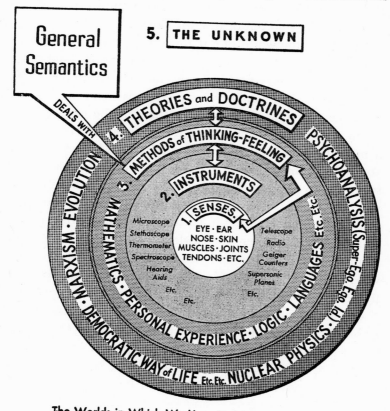

The Worlds in Which We Live (Copyright, 1948, J.S.A. Bois.)

life. I am one of these Smiths, so are you. As I go on describing my own world, fill out in imagination each concentric circle with the data that apply in your own case. Keep reminding yourself that these circles are intended to mirror a space-time fullness: they are intended to picture your world of yesterday, of last year, of years ago, concurrently with your world of today and of years to come.

These circles refer to so many subworlds, which, taken together, constitute my total world, the "universe" within which I move and out of which I cannot go.

Circle 1 is the world of our *senses*. Our first acquaintance with what is going on outside or inside our skin takes place by means of sensory nerve-endings located within our body. Whether we count only five senses, as is done in common parlance, or count twenty-two of them as the psychologists claim, we can easily admit that our grasp of what is going on is mediated and limited by them. What you have seen since you were an infant to this moment is not exactly what I have seen; what you have tasted is not what I have tasted; what you have heard is not what I have heard; what you have felt, smelled, and experienced in various ways is not what I have experienced. Your sensory world is not the same as mine. Yours is limited and mine is too. The sensory worlds of your wife, of your children, of your brothers and sisters, of your friends and acquaintances do not coincide with yours.

Our sensory experience may precede or follow knowledge from other sources. Before I saw the Grand Canyon, I knew about it from pictures and word descriptions. But my first-hand acquaintance with its awe-inspiring beauty was different from what I knew beforehand. Before I actually felt the bumping of a plane in choppy weather, I had been told about it, but the experience added something to that verbal knowledge. Whatever I am told of things that I have not experienced directly is translated automatically by me in terms of my own sensory experience. I try to imagine what it is *like;* I graft it to some sensation already recorded in my own nervous system. This world of senses includes not only what I perceive but also what I can manipulate with my un-aided body powers.

The Smiths who lived in caves and the Smiths who live the life of a primitive in some distant parts of the world have similar sensory equipment. In some cases I understand that they use it with finer discrimination than we do. But they miss many things that we can observe because they do not have the instruments that we have; they fail to achieve what we can achieve because they have no machines to multiply their own strength or harness the forces of nature.

This brings us to consider what I call the world of *instruments*. What we can perceive and do by means of tools, instruments, and machines expands our world way beyond that of the primitive Smiths. There are the instruments of perception, like the microscope, the telescope, the compass, the Geiger counter, the spectroscope, and the thermometer. There are the instruments of action, like the automobile, the airplane, the gadgets in our homes, and the machines of industry.

Review in imagination what you have experienced and achieved by means of instruments. Make sure that you limit your enumeration to what you actually know from personal experience. Do not confuse descriptions in books, illustrations in magazines, scenes from motion pictures or television, with your first-hand experiences. Is that extended world of yours identical with mine, with anybody else's? Of course not. So, we can add this accumulated world to that of the senses and admit that both, separately or in combination, are not the same for each Smith.

I call the next world of personal experience the world of our *methods of thinking-feeling*. You notice that "thinking" is hyphenated with "feeling." In the light of what we saw in the semantic reaction diagram, we could add the bodily habits and the electrochemical activities of areas A and X. Each one of us has a way of reacting to what goes on that is very special to him. I am referring here to a very complex process that is habit-forming and gives a distinctive pattern to our dealings with people and things. This can be described as the world of "mental" and "emotional" tools.

A few of these tools are listed on the chart. We use mathematics to figure out problems. Some problems are beyond us because we have not the tools to solve them. We depend on past experience and acquired knowledge to guide us in new situations. We use the logic of deduction and induction, we talk things over with ourselves or with others. We graph trends on statistical charts, we draw maps and diagrams. With these devices we interpret the experiences accumulated in circles 1 and 2. We explain what has happened, we guess what is likely to happen, we decide what to do, we communicate with one another. Some of these methods are conscious: we had to learn them and practice them. Some are unconscious: we were conditioned to them without ever realizing it. All are man-made to some extent, although we are apt to take them as "natural," as "normal" mechanisms of human nature.

Are there two of us whose past experience, habits, methods of thinking, emotional reactions, purposes, training in mathematics and logic, or practice of language, are identical? If you have the experience of a few years of married life, don't you see what I mean? Are you and your wife living in a semantic world that is the same in all respects?

Circle 4 is an expansion of circle 3. With our personal methods of thinking-feeling-behaving, and with the data that come from circles 1 and 2, we build *theories* that occasionally harden into *doctrines*. We also assimilate doctrines that are prevalent in our cultural environment. Some persons do just the opposite: they go for the unusual, the esoteric, the heterodox, but the mechanism is the same. Nobody is without doctrines, metaphysics, or some system of values. These doctrines may or may not withstand the crucial test of experience. Even when they appear consistent with experience, they remain man-made theories, inadequate in revealing the world of the limitless Unknown in which we float. Each one of us has his own ring of theories and doctrines that encircles and limits his own world.

Of the world of the Unknown little can be said, except that it is also different for each individual. For the teen-ager who poses as a Professor Know-All, the Unknown seems a thin, negligible, hazy band of mist. For the scientist, conscious of his limitations, the Unknown spreads in all directions into infinite vacuity. The extent of your Unknown may be measured roughly by the questions you ask yourself. No two people ask themselves the same questions. They are not trying to expand their individual worlds in the same areas.

The arrows on the chart are intended to show how subworlds 1, 2, 3, and 4 interact. To a blind man the microscope is of no use; to the color-blind the spectroscope is a mystery; to the man who has no ear for music a concerto is just noise. Our instruments are calibrated according to our methods of counting. Our institutions are the embodiment of theories and doctrines. Our personal world is bounded by our life philosophy (circle 4), and it takes a rocket-like mind to break through the iron ring of the culture into which one was born. Anything that comes from outside to break through the theories and doctrines that hold my world together (circle 4) is apt to provoke a "cosmic" resistance, a "life-or-death" reaction, for the crumbling of my individual world is indeed the end of all things, as far as I am concerned.

We can draw many conclusions from this analysis. Here are a few:

1. We have no common world. Each person has his own, to which he responds in his own way.

2. The similarity of our worlds depends upon the similarity of our experience, culture, language, and philosophy of life.

3. People can get along together to the extent that their worlds overlap. As a bright boy once said to his father, "The trouble with the old generation is that it does not belong to the young generation."

4. A common outlook on life (circles 3 and 4) is more powerful than a common sensory experience (circles 1 and 2) to bring about a merging of our worlds.

5. A philosophy (circles 3 and 4) that is adequate to integrate my world may not be adequate to integrate yours. Unless I become sensitive to your views and values, and you to mine, we shall remain apart, each within the steel ring (circle 4) of our own semantic world.

CHAPTER XIII

Worlds of Processes

✳ You are in your world, and I am in mine. Yours came into existence when you were born, say thirty years ago, at a time when mine had been going on for as many years. Mine will come to an end at a time when yours will probably continue for many more years. In the time dimension, our two worlds do not coincide. The First World War is part of my "today," of my life experience, of the events I have lived through. For you, it is "history," something you read about, something that lies outside your time universe.

In the space dimension, my world began in the southeastern part of Canada. If we had a globe in front of us I could show you where it has spread from that point, east to England, France, Switzerland, and Italy, south to the Mexican frontier and a bit beyond, west to the Pacific coast from San Diego to Vancouver, and not very far to the north. If in your turn you trace the boundaries of your own world in space, you would put its origin elsewhere, in Toronto, New York, the Middle West, or in some spot far distant from here. From this starting point, your space world might overlap with mine here and there, and it might spread over areas that I never expect to reach. In the vertical dimension I drove to the summit of Mount Evans, and flew a few thousand feet higher; below the ground I went down a mine shaft of about one thousand feet, and never dived very deep under water. How far did you go in either direction? Are you of the generation that will someday enjoy space travel?

Different as they are, our worlds have points of contact. Otherwise, you could not read what I am writing now. In time, we may exist in the same calendar years; in space we may have traveled through the same cities; we may even meet somewhere. In the space-time fullness that extends right across the galaxies, through history, before and beyond, I see your individual world and mine as "island universes" floating as fields of energy in a larger universe of existence.

I see similarities in your world and in mine. We communicate because our worlds have so much in common. Let us consider together some of these common features, as revealed by our brothers in existence, the Smiths who work for us in the field of science.

They say that we live in a world of processes. This is a simple, innocent-looking statement that never made much of an impression on me until I stopped and meditated upon it.

When we observe things with our senses unaided by instruments, we are struck by the evident solidity and permanence of almost everything. Here is the table, the wall, my hand, and so forth. This level of observation is called the *macroscopic* or gross level. That is the way the universe appeared to primitive man; that is the way it appears to the untutored mind of today. Our language, which was coined in the days when such a view was prevalent, contains a considerable number of words and expressions that are in accord with this static view of the universe. We speak of *things, objects, matter, solids, substances;* have adjectives, such as *permanent, stable, motionless, rigid,* that imply immobility; we use verbs that refer to long-lasting and unchanging events, such as *persist, dwell, stand, remain, endure,* and the like.

Even in the days when this static view based on gross observation was the common belief, there were some thinkers, such as Democritus, Heraclitus, and Lucretius, who claimed that the apparently unchanging face of Nature was hiding a restless process. But their theories did not sink very deep into popular consciousness. They themselves believed that the change was due to the motion of fine particles of matter, indestructible and solid, which they called "atoms," or "indivisibles." They pushed solidity and material permanence way down to the fine unseen world, but they felt it was there, at the bottom of things.

With the invention of the microscope and the advances in chemistry and physics, we came to a second level of observation, which we may call the *microscopic level*. Things that used to be considered solid proved to be full of holes through which x-rays could travel, the movement of molecules became evident, and the notion of a universe in motion made further headway. But the belief in hard particles remained practically unchanged in the popular mind; it was even slow to disappear in scientific literature. Even today, we speak of particles when we refer to electrons.

This notion of particles (meaning solid bits of matter) cannot stand any longer. We come to the *submicroscopic* level, past the realm of instruments, into a world that can be surveyed by mathematical analysis and nothing else. Experiments have confirmed beyond reasonable doubt that this world exists. In it, energy and motion reign supreme. Matter is energy. The basic stuff of our restless universe is motion, action, change, process, or whatever you care to call it. The atom is not made of solid bits; its center is a packet of energy. We have learned to turn loose this energy. The thunderous bang of the atom bomb ushered in a new age. Solid matter was an illusion. As Einstein suggested, we have to adopt a new way of thinking about the universe and ourselves if we want to adapt our behavior to what we know is going on.

Stability, solidity, and permanence were quite acceptable in the world of the Greeks and the Romans, when civilization moved so slowly that many generations would come and go before a really new discovery was made or some spectacular change occurred. Since the advent of modern science twelve generations ago, and especially since the industrial revolution of six generations ago, techniques, institutions, and theories have been changing at an ever-increasing pace. Within my own life span, I have seen more change in our way of life than could be witnessed by many generations five hundred years ago. To keep up with our times, we had better keep in tune with the newly discovered process-character of the universe, including ourselves.

When I entered my world, I learned to see it as made of discrete elements related to one another according to the dictates of the language forms I had inherited. I lived among clearly cut-out persons, things, and institutions. I perceived them as self-contained *units* that showed permanent or transitory characteristics. I observed them as acting and reacting in ways that scientists tried to understand, to predict, to influence, and to control. For instance, I said: "the bus (a unit) goes down (an action) the street (a unit)"; "the dog (a unit) barks (an action) at the moon (a unit)"; "XYZ and Company (a unit) have declared (an action) a dividend (a unit)"; "we (units) must preserve (an action) our liberties (units)"; "the executive committee (a unit) is holding (an action) a meeting (a unit)"; "the rumor (a unit) spreads (an action)"; "my memory (a unit) is poor (a characteristic)."

To adopt an up-to-the-minute way of life, let us try and free ourselves from these sharp categories, from these characteristics that are stuck to persons and to things, and from the linear relationships of action and reaction, cause and effect. This is no easy task, I admit. In this way of life that I am trying to describe with words I know are inadequate, I am a novice as you are. Yes, there may be a slight difference in the number of years I have devoted to it, in the frequency of self-observing experiences that I can count. But, compared to the tremendous possibilities of better adaptation that lie before us all, these differences between you and me are like differences in inches in a world measured in light-years.

In my experience, the passage from the old to the new way of thinking-feeling has been facilitated by training myself to talk to myself in terms of processes, of ongoings that are interdependent within a hierarchy of multidimensional wholeness.

I see processes within larger processes, which in turn are clusters of activity within larger galaxies of cosmic energy.

A "person" becomes a space-time process; so does a "thing"; so does an "institution"; so does a "feeling," a "thought," etc. In a world viewed in this manner, the "permanent" has much in common with the "transitory": both are ongoings that are ceaselessly different and new as I myself am new and different in the creative vortex of felt activity and passivity. This page is a slow-moving process; each of us is a process with phases of development that speed up or slow down; our present communication by means of the written word is a process which we entered freely and out of which we shall come different from what we were at the start.

As the process continues, we feel that we go on with a sense of autonomy and responsibility. By cultivating awareness, we keep alert to what is going on within ourselves and outside; we strive to manage our behavior within our area of freedom; we are conscious that what we think, feel, say, and do has a creative or distorting influence on the world we shall live in at the next moment, tomorrow, or for years to come.

CHAPTER XIV

Our Worlds from Within

✳ When I reached for the first time
the conclusion that my world is different from yours, I did
not realize fully what this simple statement implies. "Of
course," I said to myself, "we have no common world. I
see things my own way; other people see them their own
way."

At the time I was not aware that the word "things" was
just a substitute for "world." "Things" are there for me to
see, I thought, for everyone to see. They are there *objectively;*
each of us sees them *subjectively.* Each of us has a different
outlook on the world. The Germans have a word for it:
"Weltanshauung."

All this sounded so sensible to my own ears that I nearly
stopped there in my meditation, within the boundaries of
common sense, in the false light of the obvious. I thought I

was advancing, but I had gone around the whole vicious circle and I stood where I started at the beginning: there am I, and there is the "world." I see more or less of it in space and in time. You may see more of it if you have traveled more than I have. There is the "world," with so many of us looking at it from so many different vantage points. It is like a huge building that we may photograph from different angles, or to change the analogy, like a big pie, of which each of us may take as big a piece as he wishes.

This is not at all the picture I want to convey now. I claim that the distinction between an *objective world* and our *subjective outlook on the world* is one of the most misleading beliefs of common sense. We can *speak* of a world the same for all of us; we can *think* of a world the same for all of us. But our first-order experience is with our own individual, independent, and separate worlds, out of which we never go, except by a flight of the imagination, or, better said, by the distinctly human achievement (the French word "tour de force" would render better what I mean here) which we shall describe later when we study abstraction, analogy, and similar notions.

I am not concerned here with the philosophical problem of the reality of the objective world. Please, let us not brand one another with such epithets as "idealist," "*realist*," "*nominalist*," or the like. I am not developing a theory which I assert is the only right one. I am simply taking a fresh view of my experience, in order to deal effectively with a host of down-to-earth problems. This approach is consistent with many startling findings of today's psychology of perception. It may be just complementary to other approaches, who knows. But, unless we give it an honest try, we shall never know what we can get out of it.

Let us look at *myself-and-my-world* as one operational unit.

Whatever lies outside of this unit is the Unknown, the mysterious, the nonmanageable. The victims of the bubonic plague that ravaged Europe in the fourteenth century could not deal effectively with the germs that caused it, because these germs were not in their world of experience and knowledge. It was like an invasion from another planet, with which no earthly resources could cope. In the first chapter of this book, I described how a client of mine discovered his tibial muscle, which up to then was not part of his *conscious* world, the world with which he could deal.

As I give these two simple [examples, and eventually let the word "conscious" slip into my last statement, you may infer that I consider my "real" individual world as limited to what I am conscious of. I don't. Our first-order experiences can be described as semantic reactions (see Chapter VII) that involve more than conscious thinking (area C). However, it remains that my cumulative semantic reactions to my known and my unknown, that is the space-time sum of the transactions that have occurred in the operational unit I call "myself-and-my-world," constitute the only events of my own universe. In this sense, I can say that my world began with me, it grew in size and in complexity as I grew in experience. This experience spreads over all the areas of the semantic reaction diagram, from the electrochemical (area X) to the thinking activities (area C).

Within this unit that I describe as "myself-and-my-world," many things happen of which I am not conscious. For instance, I do not perceive the chemical exchanges that take place in my endocrine glands nor the electrical discharges that fire my brain cells. I know nothing of how the cosmic rays may perhaps influence my behavior. Until Freud came along, few people took into account the phenomena that he singled out, and labeled "abreaction," "complexes," and "libido." Until I read Korzybski, I took my language for granted, for something that required no study, no sophisticated awareness. As I go on making discoveries within my world, I am really enriching this very world out of the resources of my own creativeness, set into action by the impact of other "Smith-worlds."

My self and my world are one. Your self and your world are one. When I penetrate into your world, as I am doing now, I become subject to the climate of your world, to its laws and to its traditions. In your world things do not necessarily happen as they do in mine. My semantic reactions may fire one another into a pattern that has very little resemblance to the fireworks that create insights within you. You cannot assimilate my world in its entirety, and I cannot assimilate yours. To take in the whole W O R L D, we would have to assimilate all the individual experiential worlds of all the Smiths that were, that are, and that will be. This is impossible. The limitations of our symbols of expression are most evident here. In the free flight of his creative imagination, the poet does better than the scientist in his pedestrian explorations. Walt Whitman wrote, for instance:

> There was a child went forth every day,
> And the first object he look'd upon, that object
>   he became,
> And that object became part of him for the day
>   or a certain part of the day,
> Or for many years or stretching cycles of years.
> .   .   .   .
> These became part of that child who went forth
>   every day, and who now goes and will always
>   go forth every day.[1]

[1] Walt Whitman, "Leaves of Grass," in Louis Untermeyer, *The Poetry and Prose of Walt Whitman*, Simon and Schuster, 1949, pp. 346–348.

Coming back to the laborious discursive style of ordinary language, let us take our self and our world as two descriptive aspects of a totality, of a universe that is as unique as each individual Smith is unique. With this in mind, we can use the chart entitled, "The Worlds in Which We Live" (page 77) either as a picture of our world or as a picture of our own self. We may observe this "world-self" developing within the course of our own individual life; we may also use this frame of reference to observe the development of Smith$_n$, from homo sapiens to our twentieth century. Within their life span, the Smiths of today become much more powerful centers of cosmic energy than the Smiths of the Stone Age. Their worlds quickly grow into dimensions that are simply fantastic. We belong to this generation of privileged Smiths. I find it a most exciting occupation to take stock of our riches.

CHAPTER XV

The Growth of Our Worlds

✳ When I appeared in this world at
the very moment of conception in my mother's womb, a
new center of autonomous activity started operating in the
cosmos. This center drew upon the biochemical energies in
which it was floating, and transformed them into a life of its
own. Later, this energetic center came out of an almost completely passive state to a more active one. A child was born.
Since then I have continued absorbing energy, assimilating
it, transforming it, and using it to control my environment
to my own advantage. That environment has spread in
space and in time; it has become my own individual world,
of which my own self is the center.

When the seed of a plant is stirred into activity in the
spring, it also becomes a new center of activity. It draws
upon the chemical energies of the soil in which it happens to

grow. It assimilates them and transforms them according to a predetermined mechanism that it inherited in its chromosomes. But the plant is not free in space: it cannot move about by itself. It perishes if its environment does not give it what it requires. Plants are a *chemistry-binding* form of life. Their autonomous activities are within the dimensions of immediate contact, of chemical (and physical) reactions. For a short period of my existence I was limited to such a world.

Animals are free to move about. In the winter, my dog seeks a sunny spot on the rug of the living room; he does not wait for me to place him there as I do potted geraniums on the window sill. Birds fly south in the fall, and come back in the spring; they do not wait for me to cover them with straw as I do the delicate strawberry plants in the garden. My dog moves about in the house and outside the house. He reaches for tidbits when we are at the table, he raids the garbage pails on the street, he runs and jumps, he travels and explores his surroundings. His activities occur in space; he displaces himself to reach for sources of energy, for autonomous action, for sheer enjoyment of his ever-expanding world. He is not tied to a spot by roots, his autonomy is greater than that of the plant. As I grew, I shared the space dimensions with animals. We can be called *space-binders*, enriching our individual world in a three-dimensional universe.

I have lived also in a richer world than that of my dog. While Fido was lying down at her feet, my mother told me stories that made no impression on him. Fairy tales, stories and history, riddles and problems, reading and writing, prayers and religious services, all these opened vistas for me of a world that has kept expanding into the remote past and into endless perspectives of the future, branching in countless directions that are limited only by my knowledge and my curiosity. I assimilate with my brain subtle and powerful energies, notions, theories, and values that put me in a higher order of existence than is within the reach of plants and animals. I am not only a chemistry-binder and a space-binder; I am a *time-binder*.

If we look for a feature common to all forms of life, we may use the term *energy* to describe it. This term has the advantage also of being used in the physical sciences. Within the realm of living organisms, energy has the special characteristic of various degrees of spontaneity, of autonomy. If you object to my using the term "energy" to describe activities that range all the way from chemical reactions to ideas and values, let me quote you a passage from Kenneth Walker: "They [ideas] are powerful agents capable of taking possession of us and of propelling us in a direction in which, at the beginning, we had no desire to go. There are ideas so powerful indeed that they are capable of destroying us *body and soul*."[1]

The views and values expressed in *Mein Kampf* brought about the Second World War; the theories of Marx, Lenin, and Stalin have split the world in two; the metaphysics of Aristotle is still regulating the functioning of many of our present-day institutions.

I see my own world as a growing vortex of energies absorbed, transformed, and diffused in an autonomous existence of which I am conscious. This world becomes larger and more powerful with time; its development depends to a great extent upon my own initiative. The growth of my own world has gone through stages that repeat on a small scale the stages of development of the world of Western man, the

---

[1] Kenneth Walker, Venture with Ideas, London: Jonathan Cape, 1951, pp. 10–11.

cumulative world of the many generations of Smiths whose culture I have inherited.

The primitive Smith had practically nothing but his own body as a receiver and transmitter of energy. He was cloistered in the world of his senses (area 1 of "The Worlds in Which We Live," page 77), and he took ages to break into the larger world of instruments (area 2). He then multiplied the energy of his own muscles by inventing implements made of stone, bone, wood, or animal hide. He appropriated the thrust of the bow, the power of fire, the buoyancy of water, the push of the wind. At first, his voice could not carry beyond the power of his lungs and throat. He supplemented it by the tom-tom and by smoke signals. He maintained his body heat with clothes, outwitted animals in the hunt, and domesticated some of them to feed and serve him. Little by little, his world came to include the melting of metals, the wheel, the loom, ropes and pulleys. He developed agriculture, built houses, paved roads, created cities with aqueducts and sewers, and exchanged goods with distant parts of the planet.

Then came the industrial revolution, first with steam and later with electricity. In the last century and a half, the world of instruments has become the world of technology that has increased our perception and our power a thousandfold. We have visual and radar telescopes to search the heavens; microscopes that reveal the very small; x-ray machines and radar; sound moving pictures and television; automatic central heating, refrigerators and deep-freezers; communication by telephone and telegraph; transportation by ship, train, automobile, and plane; highly mechanized farming; factories that pour out manufactured goods, and stores that distribute them; service organizations that tend our needs.

The human life span has increased by over twenty years within a generation; contagious diseases are curbed. New varieties of plants are created, plastics and alloys provide new materials, animal husbandry has produced cows that give up to forty quarts of milk a day, and hens that lay eggs throughout the year.

Buckminster Fuller gives us a vivid account of man's mastery of cosmic energy when he translates it into "energy-slave units." "In addition to the energy spent from his metabolic income in 'working' his own body, one man in one 8-hour day can do approximately 150,000 foot-pounds of work. This additional work might be called his 'net advantage' in dealing with environment. The 'net advantage' potentially to be gained by each human each year, working 8 hours each of 250 days, per year, is 37.5 million foot-pounds."[2]

Whenever man obtains from sources outside his own body an amount of energy equal to what he can produce, he has at his service one "energy-slave" that works for him. In 1950, the effective energy mobilized from mineral fields (coal, oil, gas) and water power was equivalent to an average of 38 "energy-slaves" per capita of the world population. This would represent roughly the increase of man's work power by means of instruments. Compared to us, the strongest primitive was a weakling. Even if he had the same number of "energy-slaves" at his beck and call, he would not know what to have them do.

These "energy-slaves" are not distributed evenly over the face of the earth. In 1950, there were 347 of them for each living person in North America, 28 in South America, 27

[2] Buckminster Fuller, "Comprehensive Designing," *Transformation*, 1–1, 1950, pp. 21–22.

in Europe, 13 in Africa and the Mediterranean World, 2 in Asia, and none on the rest of the planet. The recent advances in Russia, China, and India may have already changed these figures considerably. But the point that I am making here remains evident: Smith, who lives in our Western culture in the twentieth century, is the center of a personal world that is very much different from the world of Smith, the primitive.

Your world and mine are set in motion, they pulsate and they are stirred by powerful energies from three sources:

1. The "élan vital," the metabolic exchanges, and the psychological drives that work spontaneously within ourselves,

2. the physical, chemical, biological, and human environment that presses upon us on all sides,

3. the growing crowd of "energy-slaves" and man-made institutions that restrict our freedom while they serve our needs and purposes.

To hold this world together and to cope with its energies, Smith has devised methods of thinking-feeling, theories and doctrines (circles 3 and 4) that we shall examine in the following pages.

CHAPTER XVI

Stages of Human Development

✳ To mobilize the physical and the chemical energies of his environment, Smith has had to do a great deal of brain work. From generation to generation he has accumulated thinking skills upon thinking skills, so that the creative power of the brain of the atomic scientist of today is greater than that of the discoverer of fire in prehistoric times. He sharpens theories that penetrate faster and deeper into the Unknown; he expands his space-time world at an ever-increasing rate.

Between primitive man and the Unknown, the contact was immediate, mysterious, awe-inspiring. At this stage, Smith had no impersonal way of interpreting what was going on within himself and outside. Things and events were what he *felt* they were. He lived in a world made after his own image, a world full of spirits who controlled plants, beasts, weather, rocks, and water, as he controlled his own body. This was the age of animism, of uncritical subjectivity, of superstitions passed on from generation to generation, of semantic reactions that worked unconditionally like animal reflexes. Smith did not count beyond his sensory span: "one, two, three . . . infinity." He believed in magic as a means of mastering nature. His theories and doctrines, if we can call them such, could be summed up as follows: "We are two, the world and me. The world is just as I sense it (see it, touch it, taste it, and hear it). The world is like me. In me there is a spirit; in the world as a whole, and in each part of the world that I deal with, there are spirits who rule. I have to come to terms with these spirits. I do so by rituals, by magic. The world becomes what the spirits and I want it to be. The superior man is the magician who knows the spirits and how to deal with them."

At this first stage of human awareness, Smith the caveman is already much above animals, but he is still very far from the degree of sophistication that his distant progeny, Smith-Einstein, will reach in the twentieth century of the Christian era. This stage has been called "primitive realism" or the "sensing stage."[1]

In the next stage, called *empiricism* or "classifying stage," Smith has become more observant and wiser. He realizes that the whims of the spirits do not account for everything that happens; he discovers some regularity in nature. He watches himself in his thinking and discovers logic, the consistent regularity of his own mind. He creates numbers, and numbers tell him something about the world; he classifies things and actions, and nature falls in line with his classi-

[1] J. S. Bois, "The Epistemological Profile and Semantic Psychoanalysis," *General Semantics Bulletin*, 1955.

fications; he draws conclusions from self-evident truths, and events follow one another in a cause-and-effect sequence according to his deductions. Wisdom has replaced superstition, the "lover of wisdom" (the philosopher) has replaced the magician. Aristotle teaches Alexander, the conqueror of the world.

Listen to the empiricist expounding his theories and doctrines in digest form: "We are now three: the world, I facing the world, and I observing myself looking at the world of which I am a part. To put order into my thinking and into the world, I classify things, qualities, and actions in the world and in me. I take this classification into account when I want to guide my behavior. My ideal is to be as 'objective' as possible, and thus to come to terms with 'facts' as they are. My actions and the workings of the world will correspond inasmuch as I start with self-evident principles and follow the rules of straight, consistent thinking. My thinking must be orderly, as the world is orderly. Both orders correspond: I count, I weigh, I measure, I look for connections between causes and effects in the world and in me. The superior man is the thinker who knows what is what, and what does what. We have objective doctrines to direct practical men."

It does not take much observation to discover that many common-sense theories of today belong to this stage of human development. For primitive Smith, things are what he *felt* they were; for empiricist Smith, they are what he *says* they are. His brain mirrors the world: to each thought corresponds a fact; to each word corresponds a thing, a person, an action, or a quality. If his thinking goes from one thought to the other according to logic, it directs him through the world from one fact to the next. Within his brain there is a miniature of the universe.

At the third stage, Smith doubts the reliability of his un-
aided senses, and he begins to question the objective value
of his classifications. Up to now he has contented himself
with common-sense experiences that he has filed away in his
memory according to their names, assuming that these
names corresponded to the *true nature of things*. Now he per-
forms systematic experiments, asking Nature sharp questions
that she will answer by a "yes" or a "no," by the success or
failure of the experiment itself. Instead of accepting the
logical statement, "the heavier the ball, the faster it falls,"
Smith-Galileo drops two balls of different weights. It is his
way of asking Nature: "Which one will fall faster?" He repeats the experiment, checks and measures. In every case
the answer is: "Both fall with the same rate of acceleration."

This is the birth of Science. Smith sees behind things and
actions the resilient warp and woof of the laws of Nature
that hold things together in measurable relations. This is the
"relating stage," the age of classical science. "I do not confer
with the spirits as did the primitive," says Smith the scientist. "I do not deceive myself as did the metaphysician
who took his own voice for the answer of Nature. I ask Nature
definite questions, and Nature gives me clear-cut answers. I
translate these answers into mathematical formulas that
project my conclusions into the Unknown where I discover
other facts that Nature has kept hidden since the beginning.
I geometrize the problem and I share the secrets of God, the
Great Architect of the Universe. The superior man is the
experimenter-mathematician, the man who expresses relations in formulas that reveal how the properties and the actions of men and things follow measurable sequences. These
formulas open new vistas into the Unknown: the pencil of
the mathematician directs the telescope of the astronomer to

the location of Neptune, the unknown planet; by juggling with figures, Mendelyeev determines the atomic weight and the chemical properties of elements that nobody has ever analyzed in a laboratory. This world is an immense machine where rigorous determinism reigns supreme. None of its secret workings can escape forever the skill of Smith-the-Scientist."

When the man-in-the-street thinks of science, he has this type of classical science in mind. "Judging from the popular magazines, science means, first, new gadgets: the most brilliant television set, the fastest jet plane, the most devastating atom bomb, and the new wonder drug curing tuberculosis or cancer or arthritis or, preferably, all of them. Further, it means scoops and freaks: the galaxies farthest away, the quintuplets, the conversion of a G.I. into a girl with a subsequent Hollywood contract. Above all, it means progress, faster cars, more labor-saving devices which give more time to study comics, to hear advertisements of washing powders via the radio, and to watch soap operas on the television screen!"[2]

In the fourth stage, Smith does not glory in the gadgets that are piling up as by-products along his course. He keeps asking Nature questions with increasing humility. He has received answers that baffled him. From these sobering experiences, he has learned that his questions were not properly worded; they were like the babbling of a child projecting his ignorance in front of learned men. He tries hard to match his own language with the secret code of Nature that he deciphers as he goes along. He proceeds with caution, realizing that a foolish question may bring about a thundering

[2] Ludwig von Bertalanffy, "Philosophy of Science in Scientific Education," *The Scientific Monthly*, November, 1953, p. 238.

answer that may destroy him and his species. And even when the answer is positive, he knows that it is couched in his own terms, the terms of his own questions, of his own frame of reference, of his own world as he has cumulatively created it through generations. The structure of his world is built of his own postulates, which he reëxamines relentlessly, keenly aware that they are relative to his own space-time relationship with the rest of the cosmos, with every unique event that he singles out for study. From his position in the biosphere, he sees gross regularities that he used to call "laws of nature." He now sees them as statistical averages that provide rough indications of probabilities. With these thinking tools, he discovers and even creates events that the Smiths of the three previous stages could not suspect.

This is the "postulating stage" of modern science, of non-Euclidean geometries, non-Newtonian physics, and non-Aristotelian epistemology. It involves the "new way of thinking" mentioned by Einstein, the complementarity described by Oppenheimer, the transactional psychology of Ames and his successors, the metalinguistics of Benjamin Whorf, the general semantics of Alfred Korzybski. Our institutions have not yet adapted themselves to this stage, and the whole world is going through growing pains that neither the magic of primitive realism, nor the dogmatic assurance of empiricism, nor the rigorous determinism of classical science can cope with. The discursive powers of the human mind will reach a point of diminishing returns unless they recognize their own limitations. If they don't, we may suffer from the hypertrophy that was the doom of many species whose fossil remains are scattered along the road of biological evolution. We have to ask ourselves the question: "Is man's brain too active for his own survival?"

The answer to this question is coming out, here and there. And this brings us to the fifth stage of human development, the "unifying stage."

When Smith looks at the world and at himself, when he formulates a theory and adjusts his behavior to the dynamic processes of the cosmos, he does not use only his brain. He *evaluates* as he theorizes. His sense of values, refined through the previous stages of his development, becomes the organ of a perception that transcends his rationalized knowledge. In fact, he eventually discovers that his most clever formulations take their origin and their significance from an immediacy of felt contact, of fusion and oneness with what is going on, beyond the dimensional limits of symbols, and without the distinction between the self and the non-self. The "knowing" of Smith-the-Scientist has a great deal in common with the "knowing" of Smith-the-Poet, of Smith-the-Artist, of Smith-the-Mystic. "There is a tremendous difference between 'thinking' in verbal terms, and 'contemplating' inwardly silent, on non-verbal levels, and then searching for the proper structure of language to fit the supposedly discovered structure of the silent processes that modern science tries to find," writes Korzybski. "Practically all important advances are made that way."[3]

As this type of knowledge becomes an awareness of inter-relatedness with everything, from blind cosmic energy to fellow human beings, it is translated in a variety of terms that range all the way from the cold analogies of science to the burning metaphors of the *Song of Songs*. Some will speak of a *"nous orekticos,"* of the individual as a node of interrelatedness; of our being as vectorial, as a being-to-another, as a being-with. Some will speak of "cotention" or merging of

[3] Korzybski, *Manhood of Humanity*, 2nd ed., p. xlviii.

the self with the phylum; some refer to altruism, to love-
energy, to agape, to a cosmic sense, to reverence for life, to
nonviolence, to love pure and simple.

By integrating this experience with his "intellectual"
development, Smith regains his balance, brings together the
mysticism of the East and the technology of the West, en-
riches the traditions of the thinkers and the scientists with the
heritage of the heroes and the saints. He soars above contradictions and conflicts into a creative peace where he enjoys
the freedom of accepted insecurity.

His world has a structure that no formulation can encompass, and he plays with his own symbolic constructs in a
spirit of easy detachment.

CHAPTER XVII

Semantic Psychoanalysis

✳ Not long ago, I had the opportunity of seeing on the screen a dramatic spectacle that filled me with a sense of tragedy. I saw life in action; I saw growth in process; I saw the actual division of a living cell and its transformation into two new independent ones.

It was a motion picture obtained by microphotography, and speeded up to give us a better appreciation of movement in time—something like those films that show you roots that worm their way into the ground, and flowers that unfold their petals and open their chalices to the sun. It showed nerve cells in full activity, expanding and contracting, moving their dendrites like arms that bent and stretched. Suddenly one of the cells went into a trance that shook it through and through; it looked as if it were going to destroy itself in a life and death struggle with some invisible inward foe. And lo and behold! Two young fresh cells emerged in its place, growing fast and merrily in the dance of life!

Growth involves destruction of the old and creation of the new. It destroys to build; it kills to preserve life and expand it. The transition from one stage of development to the next is a life and death struggle that spells the doom of the past and the emergence of new forms. We see it in the insect larva that wraps itself in a cocoon to emerge in due time as a free butterfly.

I see Smith-and-his-world as a growing cell that goes through five stages of development. From one stage to the next, the evolution is not a smooth continuous process. It is a painful and dramatic transformation, a life and death struggle, a tragic jump from what is to what is not yet, a cosmic upheaval that ushers in a world reborn. By his questions, Smith-Socrates destroyed the gods, and he had to accept death. That is the price we paid for passing from the sensing stage to the classifying stage. Smith-Galileo challenged Aristotle's classifications, and he was jailed within their walls. These in turn eventually crumbled under the inward pressure of expanding life. This tragedy symbolizes the passage from stage two to stage three. In our day, we are in the throes of death and rebirth, going from stage three to stage four, from proud dogmatism to humble uncertainty. Some heroic pioneers have gone even further and have taken for their code of life the nonviolence and the all-encompassing love that stage five requires. The strains and stresses of growth of our individual worlds, of our cultural, political, and religious worlds, are increasing in a geometric progression. To speak of the neurosis of our times is an understatement. We are cracking all over, and the H-bomb is just a symptom of our death-and-rebirth tragedy.

Let us forget for the moment these general considerations and come back to our own individual worlds. At what stage of development do I live and do you live most of the time? What is left in me of the primitive? When do I take the stereotypes of stage two as my standards to evaluate people and things? When do I see the world as a huge machine that the science of stage three can encompass and control? When do I question the basic assumptions of the language I think with, as required in stage four? When do I soar above the pettifoggings of my brain to live and behave in the consciousness of altruism?

Professor Gaston Bachelard, of the Sorbonne, has suggested a technique for that purpose. He sees it as a form of psychoanalysis, different from the accepted varieties of self-study introduced by Freud. It is not limited to the analysis of our feelings, but it attempts to cover the whole range of our semantic reactions, of our methods of thinking-feeling with respect to a particular event. We may call it *semantic psychoanalysis.*

Bachelard[1] gives an illustration of what he means by drawing a *personal-meaning* (epistemological) *profile* of two current

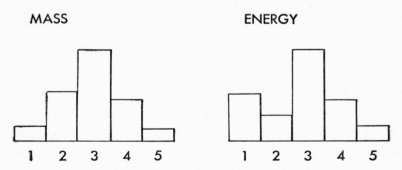

MASS   ENERGY

1   2   3   4   5   1   2   3   4   5

[1] Gaston Bachelard, *La Philosophie du Non*, Presses Universitaires de France, 1949.

scientific notions, one for *mass* and one for *energy*. He is not concerned here with the definition of mass or energy, but with his total personal reaction to these terms. The profile takes the form of a histogram made of five sections, one for each stage, with their relative heights corresponding to the relative importance of each method of thinking-feeling in the total semantic reaction that is analyzed in the accompanying diagram.

When unsophisticated people react to size and weight at the same time, they show a tendency to equate mass with bigness. This is easily demonstrated in a standard psychological experiment. The subjects are invited to weigh three cans of different size but of equal weight by lifting them with their hand one after another. They usually find that the smallest of the three is the heaviest. Why? Because their whole system, nervous and muscular, expects the largest one to be the heaviest, and it prepares itself for an effort proportionate to the size. The difference between what is expected and what is felt creates the illusion of lightness for the large one, and of heaviness for the small one.

It is difficult for even a well-educated person to overcome this primitive illusion. This means that his semantic reaction to mass involves an element of primitive realism, of uncritical yielding to sensory evaluation. At this stage, mass and smallness are contradictory terms. We confuse mass and size when we speak of masses of clouds, of massive reactions, of "the masses," meaning people.

When $Smith_n$ enters the classifying stage, he checks on his primitive experience and differentiates mass from size. He uses the scale and equates mass with weight. Observation has become controlled to some degree. Weight (or mass) is viewed as an "objective" fact, as a quality that explains what happens: heavy objects, like stones, fall to the ground, their "natural" place. The world functions as we describe it. Each element has a specific gravity that does not change because it goes with its "nature."

Whenever we take as final a clear, positive, and static notion, we think at the classifying stage. Pigs are "naturally" dirty; Negroes are "naturally" lazy; women are "naturally" intuitive, and so forth. When we can count, we are more impressed with our conclusions: the "biggest" in the world easily becomes the "best" in the world. Bachelard, a scientist, admits that his thinking about mass involves a good deal of empiricism (see diagram on page 110).

As we go from one stage to another, our notions get further away from untutored experience. At stage 3 (classical science), mass is not a static notion any more; it varies with acceleration, it is related to forces of attraction. Heavy bodies and light bodies are not differentiated by their "nature"; they obey the same "law" that experimentation has discovered and that mathematics formulates. This "law" is more "true" than the observable facts; they approximate it but they never embody it in its pure mathematical exactitude. At last we have become "scientific"; we hold Nature within the dissecting pincers of our mathematical brain!

This is the prevailing notion of mass, for Bachelard and for most people who think "scientifically." It goes with the widespread use of mathematical methods and the assurance of objectivity and precision that they give us. "Despite all the richness of what men have learned about the world of nature, of matter and of space, of change and of life, we carry with us today an image of the giant machine as a sign of what the objective world is really like," writes Oppenheimer.[2] We see

---

[2] J. Robert Oppenheimer, *Science and the Common Understanding*, Simon and Schuster, 1953, pp. 14-15.

the world as made of definite units articulated with one another in various degrees of complexity.

In stage 4, mass is not only divorced from common experience; it disappears as a distinct notion and becomes homogeneous with energy. Matter, time, and space are merely mental constructs that man creates to deal with a world of processes that slip out of the pincers of his brain. Pincers and brain are themselves carried away in the vortex. The world is seen as a network of space-time intervals filled with a fullness of point-events, each one unique in its individuality. Mass cannot be objectified in a manner independent of the means chosen for observing and studying it. Mathematics is but a storeroom of conceptual patterns. And yet, these patterns give man the awe-inspiring power to release the energies of the atom nucleus.

Bachelard is comparatively at home at this stage, and the profile of his notion of mass describes it as third in importance.

At stage 5, I part company with Bachelard. As far as I understand him, he gives it as a refinement of stage 4, with a difference that is not easy to define. This does away with the spectacular jumps that he sees between other stages. On the other hand, he introduces esthetic experience as a characteristic of stage 5, where "a kind of consciousness of totality keeps its vigil."[3] This brings us to the full unifying stage, at the point of immediate and total contact, from which all explicative notions flow through the channels of science and art. At this level where reality is only one particular case of the possible,[4] his working notion of mass is the smallest component of his semantic reaction (see diagram on page 110).

[3] Gaston Bachelard, *Le Nouvel Esprit Scientifique*, Presses Universitaires de France, p. 56.
[4] *Ibid.* p. 58

I reproduce in diagrammatic form Bachelard's notion of energy on the same page to show the differences he detected between the two. He notes that at levels 3 and 4, the two profiles are similar. At level 5, the difference is slight.

In what he calls the "infrared" part of the semantic spectrum, at levels 1 and 2, the two notions reveal great differences. His personal experience with the scale, when he worked for years as a postal clerk weighing letters and parcels, has made him keenly aware of weight and specific gravity. His personal experience with the dynamometer, as as instrument measuring energy, is very limited. This accounts for the differences at level 2.

At level 1, he notes that energy as physical or psychological pressure has a strong semantic value that distorts many of his reactions. He recognizes within himself a blending of obstinacy, rage, courage, and stubbornness, an Adlerian will to power that asserts itself frequently. "It would be interesting to delimit this concept of victorious energy; we would discover that it gives to certain thoughts an assurance, a certitude, a feeling that heightens their validity to the point of deception. The epistemological profile of Nietzche's notion of energy, for instance, might account for his lack of logical consistency. On the basis of a false notion, it is possible to build up a towering doctrine."[5]

It takes a considerable effort to pass from one stage to the next, particularly when the notion is central in our semantic make-up. There are times when a spectacular experience changes almost overnight our world of values; there are also passing insights that bring us for a short while to heights we had never known before. But if our semantic center of gravity is way down at the lower levels, we are in an unbalanced

[5] Bachelard, *La Philosophie du Non*, p. 47.

world, full of strains and stresses. "A person who exhibits different ages in his semantic development, as, for instance, 1933 in some respects, sixteenth century in others, and 300, or even 5000 B.C. in still others, cannot be a well-coordinated individual."[6]

[6] Korzybski, *Science and Sanity*, p. 149.

CHAPTER XVIII

Worlds Within Worlds

✳ On the front cover of *Life* magazine of February 27, 1956, there was a picture of an Eskimo family, father, mother, and child. They are presented as Stone Age survivors. They sustain themselves by hunting, fishing, and fowling. They have no agriculture. Their only domesticated animal is the dog, their largest social unit, the family. They live in our time-world, but they have very little in common with the commuter from our suburbs who works in an air-conditioned office, reads the daily paper on his way home, watches television in the evening, and sends his children to college. They may be extremely resourceful and skillful in the far north where I would freeze and starve, but they would be lost and helpless in Montreal or New York.

Last summer we saw one of those old cars that some well-to-do people keep in working order, and use occasionally in cross-country motorcades. It was a Cadillac that came out of the shop prior to 1910, I am sure. It was bright red, with brass ornaments shining in the sun. An elderly gentleman and his wife, dressed in the driving outfit of the time, were sitting proudly on the high seat, unprotected by windshield or top, and waving merrily to the children as they chugged through the village. They stopped at the gas station where we were filling up. "Toot your horn!" yelled a kid who was admiring the big rubber ball with the long brass tube that connects it to a bell-shaped trumpet. The gentleman tooted his horn two or three times. "That's what they all ask for—'toot your horn!'" he said with a chuckle. He took his fill of gas, turned the crank, and climbed back to his seat, shifted the crunching gears, and went along at the top speed of fifty years ago.

The Cadillac of old vintage is nearer to us than the Stone Age implements of the Eskimo, but who would want to drive it in the heavy traffic of the express-way to get to business on time?

Each stage of human development has its peculiar techniques, instruments, modes of living, bodily habits, semantic reactions and limitations. Each forms a whole that hangs together. It can be described as a different, self-contained, structured universe, made in part by man's understanding and utilizing the natural processes within his reach. Some stages are so different that they cannot blend into a harmonious whole: an Eskimo cannot remain in the Stone Age and drive a Cadillac at the same time. These two clusters of activities belong to two different cultural worlds. Anthropologists have observed repeatedly that the sudden introduction of Western man's way of life has often disturbed and nearly destroyed the survival balance of primitive cultures.

We see a similar phenomenon under our eyes when a rural family moves into the city unprepared for the shattering impact of city life. We see it in immigrants who feel up-rooted from their native environments. We see it in the child who has to grow suddenly to self-sufficiency when the family cell is destroyed by divorce. The transition from one world to another is always full of stress; it can take on the propor-tions of a cataclysm.

A searching analysis of our semantic reactions, of the total organismic meaning that events and symbols assume for you and for me, reveals that each of us does live simultaneously in different worlds that contrast and clash with each other. We are torn asunder, we harbor conflicting tendencies, we live in a house divided against itself. With respect to one single notion, we may react at one time as the primitive of stage 1 (see diagram, page 110), and then as the relativist of stage 4, and back as the empiricist of stage 2.

When this happens on vital issues, such as love, religion, security, self-image, and the like, the conflict may be so intense as to bring about a "nervous" breakdown, a sudden explosion of revolt against authority, or a bit of aggressive behavior against some individual upon whom we project the bitterness of our personal misery. We are continually stirred by milder conflicts due to the imbalance of our semantic reactions. They may not develop into dramatic tragedies, but they sap our vital energies, confuse our thinking, produce anxiety, and damage our bodily health.

Semantic psychoanalysis is a method of assessing these variances in our semantic reactions. We saw how Bachelard derived from his analysis of the term "energy" a clearer pic-ture of the obstinacy, the rage, the courage, and the stub-bornness that blend within himself to constitute the mental vigor apparent in his writing. I am very much tempted to see a ·relation between this fighting attitude and the unusual title of one of his books, *La Philosophie du Non*, which could be translated into English, *The Philosophy That Says "No" to All Philosophies and to Itself.*

In my practice as a business consultant, I have found it useful to determine roughly at what stage most of a man's thinking happens to be. Business may mean the unsophisticated play activity of a child who sells homemade lemonade to the passers-by. He has a vague notion of his costs, and the money he takes in is the measure of his profits. I remember the village general merchant of my younger days who lived on what he sold, unconcerned with turnover, and accumulating on his dusty shelves articles that remained there for years. When he took stock, it was sufficient for him to know that he had lived in relative comfort. The balance that he had in cold cash, plus a rough estimate of what people owed him, was the measure of his prosperity. He was in business at the primitive stage.

Business at stage 2 is focused on figures, bookkeeping and statistics. We read about it in financial pages, in declarations of dividends, in direct comparison between the sales of last year and this year, in overall figures that provide no analysis of the component factors of success, growth, or recession.

At stage 3, a more complex cost accounting comes into play, and the relations between market research, advertising, merchandising, production, and administrative overhead are taken into account. At the organizational level, functions are specified and interrelated; production is studied scientifically; there may be job evaluation, work simplification, mechanization of office procedures, and personnel selection.

At stage 4, the organization enters an even more fluid

condition. It becomes more responsive to the changing general economy. New products are added that have little in common with the staples of previous years, the whole system undergoes a revolution, sales organizations may go into production, new merchandising operations are created, managers become generalists, highly trained specialists push forward with research in the basic sciences from electronics to group dynamics and sociometry.

In stage 5, we see the creators of new enterprises who have the genius of feeling, as it were, the pattern of things to come. Their semantic reactions seem to be tuned to the unexpressed wants and desires of humanity on the march, and they create as they go the conditions which will give shape to the growth of our economy. Some of them become living symbols of irreversible change. For instance, a representative of this stage was Henry Ford, who introduced the era of the automobile for the common man.

Now, here are three top executives in three different firms, Al Jones, Fred Brown, and Jack Smith. When I listen to Al Jones, I recognize a recurring theme in most of his statements. "We are in business to make profits," he says. And profits for him are centered in stage 2, that of the balance sheet taken as the adequate picture of what is going on.

Fred Brown does not ignore the overall figures, but his center of interest is in stage 3. "My job is to perpetuate this business and to expand it," he repeats in some form or other. He is concerned with the streamlining of methods and procedures, he looks for personnel techniques that have produced results in similar organizations, he keeps an eye on his competitors, he attends the meetings of professional associations where he exchanges views and experiences, he reads technical magazines and business publications, he may ask for the services of well-established consulting firms.

Jack Smith has gone through these stages, and he easily keeps abreast of whatever appears within them that lightens his task and frees his initiative to push forward. He may say, "Our business is determined by the customer," or "Our function is to serve the client." He is not tied to anything definite or unchanging. He may or he may not have the glowing spark of the genius of stage 5, but he has some vague intuition that nothing stays put in this world, and he searches boldly on all fronts of his enterprise. He does not imitate; he creates and takes the risk of innovations in design, in production, in merchandising, in personnel development, in research of all kinds. He is not limited to figures that tell of the past; he is not hamstrung by methods that were safe yesterday and may prove inadequate today or tomorrow; he sees his function as a ceaseless renewal of patterns of operations in a space-time world of processes.

There may be an infinite variety of combinations of the types I have just outlined. You have the stage 5 genius who thinks as a super shop-machinist, and who ignores the figures and organizational techniques of stages 2 and 3. You have the creative inventor of methods and techniques who appears one generation too early, and disregards the financial common sense of the pluggers of stage 2. You have the system addict of stage 3, who lets himself and his organization become clogged with techniques, methods, and committees.

For a man who lives at stage 2, a project at level 3 or 4 will sound like useless theory, wild and dangerous. To the man who expects a cure-all from the operational techniques of stage 3, it seems a waste of time and money to invest in the individual development of his key men as required in stage 4, For the creative manager who functions at stage 4, a managed-expenditures budget and long-range objectives are of prime importance.

We have noticed that there is in most cases a close relationship between a man's general cultural development and his tendency to function at one stage rather than another. Unless he has reached stage 4 in some type of activity, Smith does not really belong to the growing world of today. He may drive with pride his Cadillac of 1910, not suspecting that it does not compare with the Ford or the Chevrolet of 1956.

CHAPTER XIX

Awaking to My World

✳ The alarm clock was set for 7:30
A.M. At 7:00 I woke up. It was already bright, but I did not
feel like getting up. I looked at the clock. "Thank God," I
said to myself, "I have another half-hour." I turned around,
felt how comfortable it was to stretch in the warm bed, and
slid back into sleep, dead to the world, silent to myself, floating unconsciously in a world of processes.

Then, "Drring!" went the alarm. I woke up, this time for
good. Step by step I came back to life, reëntering my world,
reassuming the consciousness I had let slip half an hour
before.

Let us observe attentively what goes on when this happens.
It may give us some clues as to how we relate ourselves to our
world. Waking up is a repetition of being born. We come to
life every morning; each day we enter the world anew.

If you look at the chart entitled "Levels of Abstracting"

Levels of Abstracting (Copyright, 1949, J.S.A. Bois.)

(page 124) as we go along, you may form a picture of what I am trying to describe. From this picture, as from a visual theorem, we can draw all sorts of useful conclusions.

First, don't worry about the title of the chart. What I mean by "levels" will become clear as we proceed. As to the word "abstracting" itself, there is nothing mysterious about it. It is intended to mean that we never pay attention to everything that hits our senses at a particular moment. By "moment," here, I mean a very small fraction of a second. As I write this, I do not pay attention to the ticking of the clock. When I listen to the clock I am distracted, for a very short moment I admit, from my writing that goes on almost automatically. When I try to observe many sensations simultaneously, I find it difficult to hold them all in focus with equal vividness. Some grow faint while others grow clear; they do not stay put with equal intensity; if I try to follow more than four or five of them at the same time, I become tired, and drop most of them.

Stop right here and make a simple experiment, similar to the one I am making now.

I shall describe a few sensations of which I shall try to be clearly aware, driving them in front of me, as it were, like so many horses that I see and control individually.

> Sensation 1: I look at the *point* of my pencil gliding on the paper.
> Sensation 2: I look at the *shadow* of the pencil that follows its movements.
> Sensation 3: I listen to the *tick* of the clock.
> Sensation 4: I feel a *pain* in my neck.
> Sensation 5: I hear the *howling* of the wind outside.
> Sensation 6: I smell the *coffee* that is brought in for the morning break.

Here I must stop, because my team of sensations has become unmanageable. I simply cannot hold so many in clear focus all at the same time. From the smell of coffee, I can pass to the howling of the wind very quickly, but I notice that the pain in my neck, the tick of the clock, the point and the shadow of the pencil are lost momentarily in the process. In fact, I doubt very much if I can be aware of more than one sensation at one instant. The light of my awareness is like the beam of the searchlight that scans the night at the airport; it is not like the sun that throws light on everything. Sometimes I may observe many things all at once in a flash of insight, but this is more like the flash of lightning in a dark night than the steady light of day.

Well, all this digression is to help us realize that your and my conscious sensory relation to the environment is made of the rapid succession of pointed, discontinuous, and shifting contacts. Our feeling of continuity and relative stability comes from elsewhere.

If, at each short moment, I am conscious of only one sensation, or of only a very few sensations, it is clear that at each moment I miss more than I observe. By moving fast I fill in the gaps, but the picture I build within myself is static compared to the cascading flow of experiences out of which it emerges.

When I say that I am *abstracting*, I mean to describe this phenomenon with one word. I *abstract*, that is, I am aware of one sensation at a time. I pick them one by one, neglecting thousands of other impacts on my senses that are simultaneous with those I observe.

Our contacts with the world around us are so many acts of abstracting. We cannot take in consciously everything that happens within our sensing range at any given moment, and a great many processes that affect us are beyond the reach of our senses. For instance, I cannot be aware of the chemical exchanges that go on within my blood stream and within the cells of my muscles. When we form a picture of what we observe, we are taking still pictures of each element or of each group of elements that we can fixate in rapid succession. While we are doing this, the processes that we are analyzing keep going on without stopping, and our pictures are out of date the minute they are taken. We combine them, more or less consciously, and their assemblage is meant to correspond as nearly as can be to the process that is going on. This composite picture has a tendency to remain static and rigid. To "abstract" means to leave out certain features of a situation, to register only those that are relevant to our needs, our purposes, or our habits.

We do this all the time. When you listen to a speaker, you neglect the other noises that impinge upon your eardrums. When you drive your car in heavy traffic, you cannot examine the shop windows. When you want to thread a fine needle, you concentrate on this and neglect everything else for the moment.

Now, let us go back to the chart. The lower half is covered with a great number of very small dots that blend together in shades of gray. These dots represent the innumerable processes that make the space-time plenum in which we float. When I am asleep, my world is a silent world of processes, and I see myself as one of these small dots, indistinguishable in the gray texture of the cosmos.

Suddenly, an explosion occurs, like the birth of a new star. My small dot opens up: I wake up from my sleep; I become conscious. This is represented in the lower left of the chart by the white patch marked "Smith-a1," (Smith-abstracting-at-the-first-stage). In some mysterious way, Smith has detached himself from the swarm of dumb processes. How did he do it? By responding to the impact of some other process, within his own skin or from outside. Scientists call this process that stirs me into awareness a "stimulus." On the chart I represent it by a small white patch, "Pn.t" or "Process-number-so-and-so-at-a-definite-time," in immediate contact with Smith who abstracts it as he abstracts his own self from the sleeping world.

From this primitive experience, Smith passes immediately to a second stage of responsiveness, of abstraction, if you will. We see him in the following white patch, S-a2 (Smith-abstracting-at-the-second-stage). The original sensation is translated into reflexes, reactions, and feelings, that are not yet expressed in words, inwardly or outwardly. If the experience is entirely new, he may not have words to describe it, but it is there just the same, within his organism that has been stirred up by it.

At the third stage, S-a3 bursts into speech. He describes to himself, or he says out loud: "Seven-thirty! Darn that alarm!" or something similar. From the silent, organismic level, he reaches for words and symbols at the verbal level. When he does this, certain nervous processes take place within him that are different from the initial experience, but are somewhat related to it. The words start a chain reaction of their own, from "description" through "Class 1, Class 2, Class 3, Class 4" on to a limitless "Class n," or final conclusion, while the nervous and electrochemical processes within Smith's organism pass from S-a3, S-a4, and so on, to S-an.

I am awake, fully awake. The world of my words, "ideas," theories, doctrines, and prejudices has started functioning at the verbal level as my organism has been stirred at the silent level.

Past experience, habits, and language will tend to rule over my abstracting all during the day. I shall see what I am trained to see, hear what I am trained to hear, and understand what fits with my previous knowledge.

Those posters (Class 1, Class 2, Class 3, and so on) that stand up in the air at the verbal level, represent the long-standing ideas, concepts and categories that we have acquired through life. They are like powerful machinery set into motion by our own reactions at the silent level. They follow their own laws and they feed back into our functioning self the orientations, attitudes, conclusions, and decisions that regulate our way of life.

A few of them come from our own experiences. Most of them come from the experiences of others, from the scientists, the philosophers, and the moralists that gave a definite pattern to our Western culture. We received them from our parents, from our teachers, from books, magazines and newspapers, from advertisements, from radio and television programs, from sermons, from cartoons, from all the channels that pour upon us the accepted values and meanings.

When I wake up in the morning, I wake up in and with my world of yesterday, of the years before, of the generations from which I inherited the life of my body, the life of my heart, the life of my mind, the life of my spirit.

Walt Whitman had a vision of this when he wrote:

> Brain of the New World, what a task is thine,
> To formulate the modern—out of the peerless grandeur
>   of the modern,

Out of thyself, comprising science, to recast poems,
    churches, art,
(Recast, may-be discard them, end them—may-be their
    work is done, who knows?)
By vision, hand, conception, on the background of the
    mighty past, the dead,
To limn with absolute faith the mighty living present.

And yet thou living present brain, heir of the dead, the
    Old World Brain,
Thou carefully prepared by it so long—haply thou but
    unfoldest it, only maturest it,
It to eventuate in thee—the essence of the by-gone time
    contain'd in thee,
Its poems, churches, arts, unwitting to themselves, des-
    tined with reference to thee;
Thou but the apples, long, long, long a-growing,
The fruit of all the Old ripening to-day in thee.[1]

---

[1] Whitman, "Leaves of Grass," *op. cit.*, p. 412.

CHAPTER XX

Finding My Way in My World

✳ When I wake up in the morning I enter a double world: 1) the world of "natural" processes, and 2) the world that Smith made and rules. The world of "natural" processes is the *silent* world, the world that goes by itself; the world that Smith made is the *verbal* world, the world of science, religion, art, industry, and culture. When Jacques Cartier woke up on the first morning of his visit to Hochelaga, he woke up to a world of nature barely touched by the hand of Smith-the-Indian; when I wake up and drive to the city over Victoria Bridge in the morning, I enter a world that is mostly man-made.

These two worlds form a whole that I cannot tear apart. They are my world of 1956, the world I inherited from the Smiths that were here before me, the world that we, the Smiths of my generation, shall preserve, spoil, or improve, to pass it on to our children, the Smiths of tomorrow.

These worlds are not only out there for me to observe at a distance. They reach into my very vitals, body and soul. I am one with them; they are one with me. All three of us constitute the space-time operating unit, which I already described (page 90) as "me-and-my-world."

When we want to understand what goes on in the world of nature, we study physics, chemistry, biology, geology, meteorology, and other natural sciences. When we want to understand what goes on in the world of man, the verbal world that Smith made, we study cultural anthropology, history, economics, linguistics, psychology, and the other behavioral sciences.

When we want to understand how Smith goes about building his own verbal world, we are faced with a very difficult task. I have approached this problem from different angles so far. We have seen that words are tools that increase and control our thinking activities; we have followed the progress of the successive generations of Western Smiths as they passed from the sensing stage to the postulating stage. In the previous chapter, we observed Smith waking up from the silent world of sleep to the active world of awareness. Let us advance one step further in our explorations.

Personally, I like the notion of *abstracting* as a guiding directive in my investigations. I have used it like a compass that tells me in what direction I am going, and prevents me from turning in circles.

Now, let us examine together this notion of *abstracting*. If we want to use it as an instrument in our explorations, we had better know how it works. We must learn how to interpret the readings we get from it. And, what is most important, we must give it an honest try before objecting to some of its features.

I insist on the last point: give it an honest try before saying that it is no good. For this instrument will not do things that you may want it to do; it will ignore certain landmarks that you consider indispensable. For instance, abstracting does not distinguish between mind and body, between the physical and the mental, between senses and brain, between the unconscious and the conscious. It takes care of all that, but in a way that is different from what you expect.

Moreover, the words "abstracting" and "abstraction" are not used here with *exactly* the same meaning you will find in dictionaries or in books on logic. Their meanings here have a good deal in common with those definitions, but they do not fit them like hand in glove. So, watch for the differences as we go on using them.

We already saw Smith waking up in the morning, and *abstracting* with his senses one bit of reality at a time, combining these bits into a picture that always lags behind what is going on. When Smith does this—and he does it all day long—we say that he *abstracts*, he picks discrete elements, transforms them, and integrates them in a structure of his own making.

We may go back to the silent level and observe Smith in his sleep, and find that he abstracts even there, without waking up. Suppose he is a sound sleeper. You tickle his foot, and he withdraws it, with or without a grunt. When I say that he abstracted your tickling, I mean that, of all the various contacts that impinged upon his skin at that moment, his nerves and muscles paid attention to this particular one and responded to it. He picked a discrete element of the situation and interpreted it as a sign to move his foot.

When the children were young, my wife would go into a sound sleep that the noises of the street would not disturb.

But let Johanna or Leonard breathe heavily, or make any other unusual sound, she would wake up and tiptoe to their rooms to find out what was the matter. She had abstracted a sound among many others that she ignored, and had interpreted it half-consciously.

You drive your car, and you suddenly feel vaguely that the hum of the motor or the rumbling of the body is not the same as usual. You abstract this change, and you try to interpret it. You come home, and you fail to abstract the new hairdo of your wife. You play chess and you fail to abstract the knight that is ready to jump sideways. You read this page, you get bored, and you fail to abstract a key word I put there for a purpose, and so on, and so on. Do you begin to see what I mean?

Abstracting covers also a great many activities at the mental level. There, it corresponds roughly to "generalizing," "classifying," "summarizing," and so forth. We pick one feature that we consider as common to many objects, and we give to all of them a common name because of that common feature. "Anthropological studies show clearly how the degree of 'culture' among primitive peoples can be measured by the orders of abstractions they have produced. Primitive languages are characterized particularly by an enormous number of names of individual objects. Some savage races have names for a pine or an oak, but have no tree which is a higher abstraction from pines or oaks. Some other tribes have the term 'tree,' but they do not have a still higher abstraction 'woods.' It does not need much emphasis to see that higher abstractions are extremely *expedient* devices. There is an enormous economy which facilitates mutual understanding in being able to be brief in a statement and yet cover wider subjects."[1]

[1] Korzybski, *Science and Sanity*, p. 377.

Let us now describe various types of abstraction. I am not ready to offer them as sharp and mutually exclusive categories. They may not cover all cases that come to mind, and they probably overlap to some extent. As they stand, they have proved useful to me.

Nominalistic abstracting. This is the ordinary process of naming and classifying, from the individual to the more and more general. "Mickey" is the name of the children's pet. We may describe him as a "spaniel" (a term of higher abstraction), or as a "dog," a still higher term, or as an "animal," a term higher still. As we go from one order to the next, we describe the individual Mickey less and less, but we can generalize better and better about spaniels, dogs, and animals.

Objective abstracting. This is the process of naming larger units that actually contain smaller units which we group together. For instance, we may go to higher and higher orders of abstraction by speaking of individuals, families, communities, and nations; and similarly with machine, factory, company, industry, or with words, statements, paragraphs, pages, books, library.

Relational abstracting. In this case, we abstract the *relations* among particular units rather than their *group character*, as we did in objective abstracting. This is the case of scientific abstracting. For instance, the formula $a^2 = b^2 + c^2$ is an abstraction of the unvarying relations among the three sides of the right-angle triangle of Euclidean geometry. A great many words, such as order, relation, analogy, dimensionality, difference, comparison, transaction, and structure, emerge from this abstracting process.

Normative abstracting. In this case, I am involved in the process. I abstract the relation that obtains between an object and myself as a semantic reactor. I say that a statement is true, and from my experience with many such statements I abstract my notion of "truth." From "truth" I go on to "quality," "virtue," "the good." I build up a hierarchy of values from specific actions to guiding principles which may become "absolutes" to me.

Self-reflexive abstracting. This type is not easy to describe, but it is important. I refer here to the process by which I observe myself in action, observing my observing, thinking about my thinking, worrying about my worrying, being afraid of being afraid, and the like.

Finally, we may generalize this notion of abstracting even more, and use it to describe all processes of energy transformation in the biological realm. The plant "abstracts," "transforms," and "integrates" the chemical energies of the soil; at the physiological level our body "abstracts," "transforms," and "integrates" the proteins, the fats, and the carbohydrates of the food we eat.

Einstein notes that the term "abstracting" may lead to some confusion when it is taken to mean extraction of elements that remain identical or similar to themselves in the process. "The relation [between the abstracted concept and the first-order experience] is not analogous to the relation between broth and beef, but rather to that between the check tag and the coat that is checked."[2]

If I want to use the notion of abstracting as an instrument to guide my explorations, I must pay attention to my moving from one order to another. The rules of nominalistic abstracting forbid me to generalize about teachers from my knowledge of one or two teachers that I have met. This would be confusing the general (higher order) with the individual (lower order). In objective abstracting, I am reminded that

[2] Albert Einstein, *Conceptions Scientifiques, Morales et Sociales*, Flammarion, 1952, p. 58.

the whole, as a whole, is different from its parts taken separately. Therefore, I am not surprised if five mature men behave like immature kids when they form a committee.

Relational abstracting gives me the pure theory that never fits exactly in practice. Normative abstracting reminds me that I am always in the picture, with my hidden assumptions and prejudices, when I speak about "honesty," "goodness," "beauty," and the like. A full awareness of self-reflexive abstracting is more cogent still: it bids me beware of the distortions of the mirror that I hold in front of myself. It makes me think of the girl who thought she was in love with a boy, when she was just in love with love as an experience.

CHAPTER XXI

Cold Facts and Human Facts

✳ "No, Mr. Jones, there are no such things as *cold* facts," said Jack.

"Jack!" exclaimed Mr. Jones. "You are not serious! Where did you get that crazy notion? You know as well as I do that facts are facts. They are something objective on which everybody must agree."

"I am sorry, Mr. Jones, but I can't accept these old clichés any more. In his course, Dr. Bois showed us conclusively that there are no such things as cold facts. Fact is a multiordinal term, and a multiordinal term has no definite meaning."

Mr. Jones was nonplussed. He took a searching look at his young assistant, trying to detect on his face some sure indication of incipient insanity. Ever since he had returned from a course in executive methods, a week ago, Jack had come out once in a while with strange statements that shocked everybody's common sense. But this was the limit: Jack was losing touch with reality. The course had gone to his head.

Mr. Jones called me up. "Dr. Bois," he said, "I am afraid something has gone wrong with Jack. Did you notice any sign of mental confusion when you had him on your course recently?"

"No, Mr. Jones," I answered. "In fact, I think that he was one of the brightest members of the group."

"Well, perhaps he was. In fact, I have always felt that Jack is a very bright young fellow. That's why I sent him to take your course. But since he came back, he seems full of strange ideas."

"Strange ideas?" I said, "Can you give me an example, Mr. Jones?"

"Well! I don't mean to say that he does anything crazy," replied Mr. Jones. "It's more a question of funny theories that he blurts out when there seems to be no reason for them. For instance, just a few minutes ago, I told him not to pay so much attention to the opinions of the boys in the shipping department, but to dig for the cold facts, the real measurable facts of the situation. You won't believe me, Dr. Bois, but he came out with the statement: 'There are no such things as cold facts, Mr. Jones.' And, what is worse, he blames you for these funny notions."

I was on the spot, indeed. Mr. Jones was worried. Either Jack was going off the beam, or I had been preaching very dangerous theories. I invited Mr. Jones to have lunch with me the following day and to bring Jack along. He accepted.

We sat down and started with the usual generalities about the weather and business conditions. Eventually Mr. Jones opened up.

"I am afraid Jack has been misinterpreting some of your teachings, Dr. Bois. You see, I don't mind his throwing at us some new technical terms that he learned in your course. Young people like to show off, you know as well as I do. But when he comes into head-on collision with common sense, I begin to wonder."

"In head-on collision with common sense?" I queried.

"Yes," nodded Mr. Jones. "That's exactly what I mean. Jack, what did you say about cold facts, yesterday?"

Jack's face glowed with the anticipated pleasure of a good argument between Mr. Jones and me.

"Didn't you show us, Dr. Bois, that there were no such things as cold facts? That's all I said to Mr. Jones. I may have used the word "multiordinal," and I know it is—hmm—a rather special term. But I like it, and it means so much to me now that I understand the whole thing. Don't you agree?"

I turned to Mr. Jones.

"Would you give me an example of what you mean by *cold* fact?" I asked.

"Well," he said, "I can give you several. Here is one: Pierre Laval, former Premier of France, was executed for treason in October, 1945. Another one: We have a definite number of Canadian soldiers in Korea at this moment. Another one: Our product "Miraplus" is packaged in boxes that measure 2 x 6 x 10 inches. These are facts, aren't they? What is subjective about them? They are there, whether you know them or not. Your opinion about them does not change them a bit, does it?"

Jack's face did not glow any more. Mr. Jones' examples were so clear-cut and cogent that common sense was winning over "scientific" theory. I made a strategic withdrawal.

"Yes, Mr. Jones," I said, "I agree with you that these are

cold facts, independent of human opinion. As long as nobody thinks of them or reacts to them, they do not cause a ripple in human affairs. In this sense, your "Miraplus" package is the same cold fact for everybody. But does everybody react to it the same way? I know that your sales manager would like it modernized in design and color. He claims that the house-wives of today leave it on the groceteria shelves to buy competing brands. In the plant, I heard complaints that it is the only product still packaged in tin boxes, and they are experimenting with wax cartons. Your accountant is studying the cost of these changes. Your research department is considering an improvement in the product itself, and this may make you pass from tin boxes or cartons to collapsible tubes. What would you call all the thinking, the planning, and the arguing that goes on around that 2 x 6 x 10 tin box, Mr. Jones? Are these activities cold facts of the same type as the size of the package?"

Mr. Jones chuckled. "No, not *cold* facts," he said, "but *heated* arguments, as you know very well."

"And those heated arguments," I pursued, "can't we call them *human* facts, or facts that include the *cold* fact of the size of the package and a great many things besides?"

"Of course," agreed Mr. Jones, "most of my headaches come from those *human* facts. I often say that the trouble is with human nature."

"And your attitude toward human nature," I continued. "Is it not a fact? This fact includes many experiences other than the one just described concerning the reactions of many of your men to the Miraplus package?"

"Oh, yes!" assented Mr. Jones, "It is a fact that I have piles of facts to support my attitude."

"Which brings us back," I said, "to that word 'fact,' an

apparently clear but really indefinite word that means some-times little, sometimes very much."

Mr. Jones took a slow sip of coffee, and remained silent for a while. Then he spoke meditatively, as if listening to his own thoughts: "It's strange. I never looked at it that way. I thought I knew what a fact is. But now, I wonder. You have *cold* facts, of course. They are simple enough. But those *human* facts that contain other facts, that contain still other facts . . . they have me puzzled."

"We are all in the same puzzle, Mr. Jones," I said. "When we speak of a cold fact as you call it, we are really dealing more or less consciously with a *human* fact. The minute you bring a *cold* fact into the conversation, you reveal that this *cold* fact has a special meaning to you. Some way or other, you deem it relevant to the occasion, and this makes it a *human* fact. *Cold* facts are dead facts, they have to become *human* to enter our life. Now, tell me how you happened to mention Pierre Laval earlier in our conversation."

"Well," he drawled with hesitation, "this is a long story. Day before yesterday we were visiting at the Browns, my wife and I. On the wall of their living room I noticed a small frame containing the citation that made Ted a Knight of the Legion of Honor during the first World War. It was signed by Marshall Pétain. And I suddenly thought that Pétain, who was then entitled to sign citations for bravery, is now banished as a traitor, too old to be executed as Pierre Laval was in 1945. This must be how Laval came into the picture. I felt sort of bad for all those tragedies."

We finished our lunch in friendly agreement. Mr. Jones turned to Jack with a beaming smile. "You had me worried for a while, Jack," he said. "But I feel better now. If I want to keep up with you young people, I suppose I'll have to learn those technical terms that the good doctor is teaching you. What was the word you said yesterday when we spoke of cold facts?"

"I said that fact is a *multiordinal* term, Mr. Jones," said Jack as we got up from the table.

CHAPTER XXII

Multiordinality

✳ The multiordinality of terms was formulated in 1925 by Alfred Korzybski. In a paper that he presented at the 1931 meeting of the American Association for the Advancement of Science, he admitted that it was still generally unknown. The various writers who have commented on the Korzybskian methodology have not stressed this particular formulation very much, in spite of the fact that he had insisted repeatedly on its importance. For instance: "All the most humanly important and interesting terms are multiordinal, and no one can evade the use of such terms. Multiordinality is inherent in the structure of 'human knowledge.' This multiordinal mechanism gives the key to many seemingly insoluble contradictions, and explains why we have scarcely progressed at all in the solution of many human affairs."[1] Elsewhere, he reminds his readers that this

---

[1] Korzybski, *Science and Sanity*, p. 74.

144

mechanism should be explained at all stages of education: "To avoid confusion, we should have to make clear the multiordinality of terms, and to embody the recognition of this multiordinality in every, even the most elementary education."[2]

My own experience has been that, once this relatively simple notion has been mastered, its application becomes frequent, easy, and fruitful.

Multiordinality refers to the orders of abstraction that we described previously. When we move to higher orders in the process of abstracting, we pass, for instance, from the proper name "Mickey" to the breed name "spaniel," then to the more general names "dog," and "animal." There is no confusion here. To each order corresponds a different word. In objective abstracting, we also give an example where no confusion is likely to occur: individual, family, community, state, nation, and so on.

The trouble begins when we have to use the same term in many different orders. Then we may well pass from a lower to a higher order and vice-versa, without realizing that we are sliding back and forth from the particular to the general. Since a great many of the words that we use are of this type, no wonder that misunderstandings are frequent. Let us start with a simple example.

In the army, the term "unit" applies to formations of different sizes: a unit is part of a larger unit, which in turn is part of a still larger unit. Fortunately, there are specific terms for each type of unit: platoon, company, battalion, brigade, division, and so forth. However, it remains that we can make statements that will sound paradoxical if taken literally. A captain commanding a company could say to his

[2] *Ibid.*, p. 306.

lieutenant colonel, "My unit is in your unit"; and the lieutenant colonel could say to his brigadier general, "My unit is in your unit." In these two statements, we have the term "unit" at three different orders of abstraction: company, battalion, and brigade. A peculiar feature becomes evident: the lowest unit is contained in the next higher, and this middle one is both the container of the lower and part of the contents of the next higher one. This feature is common to all multiordinal terms: they refer to containers and contents at the same time. The problem is to determine which is which.

This term "unit" is also used in other contexts. We speak of units of distance, of time, and of money. In science we may take as our *unit of discourse* a limited field within a broader field. The psychologist studies the individual as a *unit;* the sociologist studies the group as a *unit;* the anthropologist studies the culture as a *unit.*

The number of words that may refer both to container and contents is legion. For instance, take the word "problem." A foreman may have a problem with an employee's grievance. He cannot solve it because this problem is part of a larger problem between the union local and management. This last problem, in turn, may be part of the more comprehensive problem of the union as a whole with a competing union or with the particular industry as a whole. This in turn may be part of the much wider problem of the economic and political condition of the country. It is evident that the word "problem" does not refer to the same total situation every time it is used here. The foreman's problem is part of the works manager's problem, which is part of the company's problem, which is part of the country's problem, and so on. At what level the problem should be tackled depends on circumstances.

The word "fact," which bothered Mr. Jones in the previous chapter, is of the same kind. We had, say, 25,000 Canadian soldiers in Korea ($fact_1$). This fact is part of the intervention of the United Nations in that country ($fact_2$). This in turn is part of the Far East situation ($fact_3$). This in turn is part of the general East-West split ($fact_4$). Where shall we stop? What is a "fact"?

During the War, soldiers were told that it is normal to experience *fear* when they jump forward to the attack. $Fear_1$ sets in motion a physiological mechanism that prepares the organism for action. But $fear_2$ of this normal $fear_1$ becomes anxiety that cripples the fighter. When these fears become generalized $fear_{3, 4, 5} \ldots _n$, you have a full-blown neurosis.

Most people *think*, but fewer people $think_2$ about their spontaneous $thinking_1$. We say that they lack a critical sense; they do not check on what they do. If they $think_3$ too much about their $thinking_2$, that is, if they become unduly introspective, they cramp their style. They cannot speak, they cannot write; they cannot make up their minds, they suffer from indecision. Where is it safe to stop *thinking* and take the chance of *doing?*

So, you see that the number of multiordinal words is legion. They are probably the most common in our language. They are all-purpose tools that we keep within reach and use for almost anything. Here are some of them: fact, situation, business, period, reality, function, cause, effect, true, false, real, to know, to speak, to hate, to love, to fear, to doubt, yes, no, etc., etc.

One of the main troubles with these words is that we cannot define them. What is a "fact"? What is a "situation"? What is "reality"? What is "love"? What is "doubt"? What is "fear"? What is "business"? If you ask me to define my terms, I am in a quandary. Yet, I know what I am talking about. That is, in a vague sort of way. You know also, but in a vague sort of way. We are both lost in the fog. You yell to me, "I am here," and I yell to you, "I am here." But, ah, me! Where is "here"?

Let us try and lift that fog. We shall do so by using what we already know about abstracting and orders of abstracting. When you tell me, "Define your terms," you invite me to reach a higher order of abstraction and to give you generalities. Instead of that, let us be more specific and pinpoint what we are talking about. Don't ask me, "What is a fact?" but ask me, "What fact are you talking about?" Then I shall do my best to describe what, when, where, how, and who. (In General Semantics, they call this to "extensionalize," or to "chain-index"). Or, you may use what the scientists of today call "operational" language and say: "What is (was, has been, will be) going on that you want to talk about?"

CHAPTER XXIII

How Clear Is Clear Thinking?

✳ If you don't mind, we shall explore
a bit further in the direction of multiordinality. It will give
us some indication of the shifting basis of most of our thinking. When we realize this, we may understand why humility
is one of the most realistic and healthy virtues.

Well, let us go back to our first example: *unit*. It can apply
to army units (platoon, company, battalion, brigade, division), to units of time (second, minute, hour, day), to units
of money (cent, nickel, dime, quarter, dollar, "grand"), to
units of discourse in science (gene, chromosome, cell, organ,
organism, or individual, group, culture). I say that the term
"unit" is multi-meaning and multiordinal. By "multi-
meaning," I want to describe the fact that this term is used
in many areas (army, time, distance), and by "multiordinal" I want to describe the fact that in each area the

term may be used at any lower or higher order of abstraction.

This can be visualized by spreading the various uses of the word in a two-dimensional array, as in the following table:

UNIT$_1^n$	UNIT$_2^n$	UNIT$_3^n$	UNIT$_4^n$	UNIT$_5^n$	UNIT$_n^n$
"	"	"	"	"	"
"	"	"	"	"	"
"	"	"	"	"	"
UNIT$_1^4$ (brigade)	UNIT$_2^4$ (day)	"	"	"	"
UNIT$_1^3$ (battalion)	UNIT$_2^3$ (hour)	UNIT$_3^3$ (yard)	"	"	"
UNIT$_1^2$ (company)	UNIT$_2^2$ (minute)	UNIT$_3^2$ (foot)	UNIT$_4^2$ (nickel)	"	"
UNIT$_1^1$ (platoon)	UNIT$_2^1$ (second)	UNIT$_3^1$ (inch)	UNIT$_4^1$ (cent)	UNIT$_5^1$ (gene)	"
UNIT$_1^0$ (army)	UNIT$_2^0$ (time)	UNIT$_3^0$ (distance)	UNIT$_4^0$ (money)	UNIT$_5^0$ (biology)	UNIT$_n^0$ (anything)

From left to right we have the multi-meaning aspects, which go from $_1$ to any number ($_n$). From the bottom up, we have the multiordinal aspects which go also from ^{1} (low order) to any order you wish (^{n}). No two units in this array have the same two indexes. They are all different. By giving the two indexes to the unit you choose to talk about, you pinpoint it with accuracy; thus you avoid confusion.

If you want to take another dimension into account, say the date, you may picture to yourself a tri-dimensional system of coördinates, and use three indexes instead of two. Again, you avoid confusion; with the three indexes you can pinpoint with accuracy the particular unit you refer to.

But, what of the word "unit" itself, the word common to all points in the array, the word that could be written with zeros as indexes: "unit$_0^0$"? What does it mean, all by itself?

Does it mean something as definite as those numbered units that spread all over the table? Of course not. Does it mean nothing? Of course not. It must mean something that makes it different from other multiordinal terms. We know, however vaguely, that "unit" is not quite the same as "fact," "reality," "situation," and other terms of that very confusing class of multiordinals.

How shall we describe that vague "something" that "unit" means, vague but different from the other "something" that "fact" means? This is no easy task. It brings us to the rock bottom of human thinking, abstracting, consciousness, awareness, or whatever you want to call it.

Yes, you will find the word "unit" in the dictionary. I have a college edition of the Winston here. Let us see what it says. "Unit: one person or thing of a number which make up a group." Fine! Now, let us look at the first word used in the definition, the word "one." The dictionary says: "One: being a single unit, being, or object." So, there you are! "Unit" means "one," and "one" means "unit"! If this is not turning in circles, I don't know what is!

The scientists have done their best to tackle this problem. They give all sorts of names to that strange, hard-to-describe phenomenon, by which we know what we mean, yet don't know how to define the term that we use. They speak of "conceptual organization," of "conceptual structure," of "patternment," of "core of analogy," and what not. That "structure" or "patternment" is something which you feel somewhere, somehow, inside you, and which you may express by a generalized tension, a movement, or a gesture, as, for instance, when you hold up your index finger to describe "unit."

Now, if you want to get the feel of our limitations as regards precise meanings, take any multiordinal word that you please, and bring it to its rock-bottom signification. You will find it a very sobering experience. You will discover that the clear mind of which we like to boast is not so clear when we go down to its depths.

Shall we give up our exploration at this point? No, let us go a bit further, or rather, roam around the place. We may find something interesting. We are not the first ones to come down here. Most sages, thinkers, and philosophers have explored this region. Some were Oriental, some were Westerners. We are Westerners by language and tradition.

Both Orientals and Westerners seem to agree that there is no common measure between language and experience (or reality). The Orientals insist on what reality *is not*, we insist on what it is *like*. They use the negative way, we use the positive. Don't ask me which way is better. I don't know. It is a matter of preference, I imagine.

Now, when you say what a thing is like, you use *analogy*. You refer to some past experience, common to most people, and you say that the new experience you want to describe is *like* this or *like* that. This is as far as you can go. If your listener has no experience comparable to yours, he simply tries to find in his own stock of experiences the one which he thinks fits best. To a man blind from birth, you cannot give the feeling of what a color is like.

Analogy is the key word here. We all use analogies. The poets are expert at it. The scientists have to use them, too, if they want to think and speak at all. "The worker in the laboratory," writes Hebb, "does not merely report and expound by the aid of analogy; that is how he thinks, also. The atom was once a hard little round particle, or later on with hooks on it. Recently it was a solar system. The classical dispute of physics about the nature of light was really asking: Is light like a shower of pebbles, or like ripples in a bathtub? The ultimate answer—Both—was one that was hard to accept. Why? Because it fitted into no pre-existing conceptions; waves are waves, and pebbles are pebbles—there is nothing in common experience that has the properties of both."[1]

The "core of analogy" that multiordinal terms evoke, the particular cluster of experiences that they bring to consciousness, that is what they "mean." Most of our thinking originates from "systematized ambiguity," from loose-fitting analogy.

Too bad for the "clear" minds!

[1] D. O. Hebb, *The Organization of Behavior*, John Wiley and Sons, 1949, p. 119.

CHAPTER XXIV

Multiordinality in Business

✳ This notion of multiordinality has proved very helpful in many practical situations. It gives a second dimension to our capacity to differentiate things and processes that go under a common name and that are easily mistaken one for another.

We differentiate in a first dimension when we imagine putting the various meanings of a word in a row, say from left to right, and distinguish one from the other by using a serial index or a verbal modifier. For instance, I may say that I made a decision, but I may want to differentiate between various types of decision, like this:

Decision$_1$, Decision$_2$, Decision$_3$ . . . Decision$_n$.

Decision$_1$ could be "decision taken on the spur of the moment"; decision$_2$ could be "decision taken after a personal study of the situation"; decision$_3$ could be "decision taken jointly with my business colleagues"; decision$_4$ could be "decision accepted by me for reasons different from those of my advisers," and so on. These various decisions have in common the fact that that they involve some action to which I agree, but they are different in the way they were reached and in the extent to which I feel they are my very own. Some may be more easily reversed than others. If I say, "When I *decide*, I stick to my *decisions*," I may not differentiate clearly enough the multi-meaningness of these words "decide" and "decision," and I hold myself to a rigid consistency of behavior that is not in keeping with the facts.

Multiordinality goes in a dimension that cuts multi-meaningness at a right angle, as we saw in the table devoted to the study of unit (page 150). Here we do not differentiate as to kind, but we differentiate as to comprehensiveness; one decision may or may not include many other decisions of a lower order. Multiordinal thinking could apply to a variety of business terms, such as objectives, management, purposes, relations, and training.

Let us take "decision-making" as an example. Decision-making describes the process of choice and action, from routine activities that fill most of our days to far-reaching plans that give orientation to our whole life. In decision-making, a man figures out—by himself or jointly with others—what has to be done, can be done, or will be done, by himself and/or others. He reaches some conclusion, initiates some action.

In all cases, decision-making involves people and things. The term "people" covers individuals, their general abilities and special aptitudes, their experience, their know-how, their purposes, their ambitions, their willingness to accept responsibilities. The term "things" covers money, physical facilities, circumstances of time and place, procedures and methods, economic conditions.

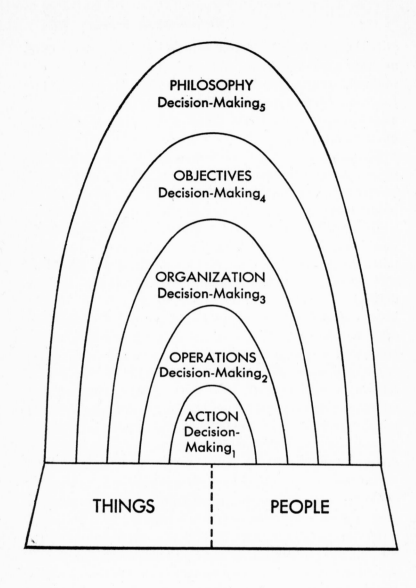

Decision-making is viewed in the following diagram of increasing spread in space and time, typical of multiordinal notions. Decision-making of a low order is contained within the frame work of decision-making of the next higher order. This in turn lies within the limits of broader and higher decisions, and so on.

Decision-making$_1$, or "decision-action." We deal here with routine or semi-routine activities. I examine regular reports, exchange information on simple facts, dictate and sign letters, approve expenses that are within the budget, and allocate work to subordinates. There is very little deliberation here: most decisions fall in line with predetermined habits. It is only when something unusual happens that I stop and think a bit longer. I may then pass to the next stage of decision-making.

Decision-making$_2$, or "decision-operations." We deal here with the planning and coördinating of a group of activities. It may be a special trip, a more important assignment, an order of unusual size, an increase in the staff, a review of salaries, a change in office or department layout, or a revision of certain forms. It may call for consultation with the people involved, a review of ways and means, a change in procedures, or a different time sequence of what has to be done.

Decision-making$_3$, or "decision-organization." Here we enter the field of organization planning, of changes likely to affect the very structure of the firm and not only its operations. We deal with the creation of new functions at the executive level, with hiring and/or promotion of key people, significant expansion or curtailment of production facilities, overall budgeting, labor negotiations—with decisions that commit the company for months or for years.

Decision-making$_4$, or "decision-objectives." We are dealing here with major decisions reserved to the Board of Directors or to the control of the majority of shareholders. They may involve the firm's whole future, its growth, its solvency, its size and place in a particular industry or the general economy. A change of the top executive falls within this category. Other examples come to mind: the creation of a new division, a merger with other companies, and the introduction of an entirely new service or product.

Decision-making$_5$, or "decision-philosophy." We are dealing here with elements that are not so easily observed as the previous ones, but they are probably the most influential in determining the fate of an enterprise. Some historical examples can be cited: for instance, Henry Ford's policy of one-man rule which reduced his share of the automobile market from two-thirds to one-fifth within fifteen years. It is hardly correct to speak of decision in the sense of change at this level, for the basic philosophy of a controlling group is so deeply imbedded in their nervous systems that it takes a cataclysmic experience to shake it off. More often, the people themselves fade out of the picture with the philosophy that has failed. It remains that decision-making$_5$ does affect all other subtypes of decision. It may or may not be explicitly stated in official pronouncements; it may be camouflaged in axioms that sound full of wisdom, but it controls everything else just the same.

Needless to say, the boundaries between these various orders of decision-making are not so sharp as they appear on a diagram. Each stage is in close relation to the others; a searching analysis of an action at stage 1 may reveal the subtle influence of stage 5. Operations (stage 2) cannot work smoothly if the organization (stage 3) is not properly structured, and so on.

However, I think that the differentiation given above has some practical value. It establishes an hierarchy of decision-making activities; it shows which ones are more important, which ones deserve a greater expenditure of brain power, time, and money.

We can visualize executive functions as cutting across the decision-making diagram at a right angle to the plane of the paper. They apply to all stages of decision-making—from routine actions to the basic philosophy of the enterprise. Stage 1 involves listening, communicating in extensional and actional language, avoiding tension and tenseness. Stage 2 calls for skill in dealing with people, obtaining their participation by means of a perceptive approach, maintaining a constant feedback from operation to direction. Stages 3 and 4 require a broader range of awareness at all levels of semantic reactions.

Stage 5 is the one where change and improvement are the most difficult to achieve. The problems raised at this stage are not specific to business and industry. They are present whenever men are engaged in activities that take root in the deeper layers of their cultural, professional, and self-preserving assumptions. Decision-making that is really significant at stage 5 involves a reëxamination of a man's outlook on the world and on himself. It means a new orientation of his thoughts, feelings, and ambitions.

CHAPTER XXV

Introducing the Structural More

✳ *Two is company, three is a crowd.*
Two and three are numbers that you can compare. Two
is smaller and three is larger, but they are both of the same
kind.

Company and crowd do not compare in the same manner.
A company is not a smaller crowd, and a crowd is not a
larger company. They are not of the same kind. One calls
for a certain type of behavior, and the other calls for another
type. A crowd is made of people, and a company is made of
people too. The crowd in this case may include only one
more person than the company. Two persons may be the
same in both cases. The time and the place may be the same,
also. But when the third person comes in and begins to interact with the first two, something happens that changes the

whole situation. The *company-character* of intimate togetherness disappears, and the *crowd-character* emerges. There has
been more than the *additive* change from two to two-plus-one;
there has been a transformation from a *twosome* to a *threesome*. Because of the presence of the third person, the first
two are affected in their relations with each other. The life
of the group has passed from one *order of existence* to a different one. Each order of existence is unique; it has dimensions of its own. The second one is not the first one plus more
of the same elements; the sameness of the elements has been
transformed too.

If you say, "There were two persons before the change,
and there is one more now," you give me a static picture of
before and after, but you do not describe the process of
change and the transformation it brought about. You count
the elements of the *company* and you count the elements of the
crowd, and you compare the numbers obtained. The numbers stand in the proportion of two to three, but the *company*
and the *crowd*, as operating units of different complexity, do
not stand in the same relation of two to three. The intimacy
of the twosome is gone; the "triangleness" of the threesome
is felt in its place.

As I meditate upon this, I realize how difficult it is to
describe with one word a process that has no distinctive
name in our language. The situation is more serious and it
becomes a threat to our sanity when the only words that we
can find in our thinking "tool chest" are so inadequate that
they make us miss the characteristic feature of the phenomenon. It is like trying to eat soup with a fork: we scarcely get a
taste of it.

Let me quote to you a few passages from Korzybski that I
consider pertinent to this problem:

If facts cannot be covered by given linguistic forms and methods, new forms, new structures, new methods are invented and created to cover the structure of facts in nature.[1]

With our present low development and the lack of structural researches, we still keep an additive Aristotelian language, which is, perhaps, able to deal with additive, simple, immediate, and comparatively unimportant issues, but is entirely unfit structurally to deal with principles which underlie the most fundamental problems of life.[2]

Linguistic and semantic researches show that the structure of all languages can, and *must*, be made similar to empirical structures; and then, also, the rest of humans can, and probably will, behave in a less silly and futile way than they have done in the past and are doing at present.[3]

It is desirable to introduce consciously and deliberately, *terms* of a *structure* similar to the *structure* of human knowledge, of our nervous systems, and of the world, involving appropriate *semantic reactions*.[4]

Conscious as he was of the radical changes that are taking place in our civilization, Einstein said somewhere that we have to adopt "a new way of thinking," and I understand that his prescription covers the human problems that Korzybski describes in the passages quoted. When I translate their statements into my own language, I say that we have to create new and better thinking tools to manage our interpersonal, intergroup, and international relations, if we want to keep alive and fulfill our destiny in the world that our technology has made more complex and more tight-fitting than it ever was. Even though we are not geniuses like the great men who created the inventions that mark

[1] Korzybski, *Science and Sanity*, p. 172.
[2] *Ibid.*, p. 265.
[3] *Ibid.*, p. 365.
[4] *Ibid.*, p. 174.

turning points on the paths of history, we must, all of us, work as hard as we can to improve the thinking tools we already possess, and experiment relentlessly until we succeed in devising new and better ones. If this is the century of the common man, the common man has to get into the act.

Well, I am quite willing to assume my responsibilities as a common man, and I presume you are. So, let us pursue our analysis and see what we can suggest.

When we think with numbers, we add and subtract. These are the fundamental operations of arithmetic, and they are wonderful as long as we remain in the world of arithmetic. The trouble starts when we unwittingly use additive and subtractive thinking in human affairs where it does not apply. For instance, it is true that two plus one make three, but it is not equally true that two persons who are joined by a third person while they are in an intimate tête-à-tête consider the third one as a mere addition to the group. Their "two-ness" is disturbed, or perhaps relieved, as the case may be. Two plus one is not a case of addition here; it is a case of total change, of transformation. And the transformation is the important feature of the process.

The word "more" that we use when we say "Three is more than two" may be the one that hides that process of transformation. Let us analyze it.

"More" is a term of comparison; it expresses a relation between two things *of the same kind*, one of which is greater than the other. It does not express clearly the relation between two things *of different kind*, one of which includes the elements of the other, but has them integrated, combined, arranged, and structured differently from what they were before. To convey that notion of restructuring the smaller unit that has been absorbed into a larger one, I suggest that we think in terms of a *structural more*. This would mean two things: 1) the second unit that is compared, in this case the *crowd*, has a greater number of elements than the first unit, the company; 2) the elements of this second unit, including the elements of the first that enter into it, are put in different relationships to one another; they are *structured* according to a new pattern.

Now, let us see how this new notion of a *structural more* fits other empirical structures of events and processes that we can observe.

A chemical compound is *structurally more* than the sum of its elements. Pure water is made of two parts of hydrogen in chemical union with sixteen parts of oxygen. This compound has not the properties of hydrogen *plus* the properties of oxygen, it has *other* properties. The compound has a structure of its own; this structure keeps the elements within a certain relationship and proportion. If you try to introduce oxygen into the water, in a proportion of more than eight parts to one, this oxygen will not be integrated into the compound, but will remain outside its chemical structure. The quantity, the relationships, and the properties of the elements are controlled, as it were, by the new structure. Water is *structurally more* than *hydrogen plus oxygen*.

We say that man is a "rational animal," or an "animal plus a *cerebral cortex*." If we say that man is *structurally more* than the mere addition of animal characteristics and reasoning powers, or *structurally more* than the addition of an animal body and a more elaborate cortex, our "mental" picture becomes more accurate. His animal qualities, taken as elements, are rearranged; they are individually related with his distinctively "human" activities. From this re-structuring emerges an entirely new "entity," a unique "nature," that is neither angel nor beast, neither "rational" nor "animal," but that obeys laws of its own "structure," of its own "make-up." This particular compound structure controls the quantity, the relationships, and the properties of the elements that enter into its constitution. If one element is isolated, and/or overdeveloped in undue proportion, we have a case of hypertrophy, of unbalanced growth of a part, that may destroy the whole organism, or, perhaps, bring about a mutation. I read somewhere this quip of an anthropologist: "Man is an ape with a brain too active for his own good." It would be interesting to study the problems of our generation in the light of this statement.

This formulation of the *structural more* applies also to a variety of situations where an increase of certain elements beyond a critical point changes the whole picture. I am thinking now of such things as the break-even point in cost accounting, of the "straw that breaks the camel's back" of popular lore, of the missing nail in the horseshoe that brought about the loss of a kingdom.

When we are aware of the structural more we are ready to take a "semantic jump" into a world of different dimensions whenever circumstances call for it.

CHAPTER XXVI

Semantic Jumps

✳ Please, don't take the *structural more* as a mere verbal form, clever or not, that we add to an esoteric vocabulary. Its value depends on what we get out of it. To get something out of it, we have to train our semantic reactions accordingly. Here is one way of doing it.

First, let us shake off the gross sensory associations from the key words we have to use. These words are "structure," "dimension," and "order." If the term "structure" evokes in your mind the solid steel girders that are bolted together to build a skyscraper, you are not completely wrong, but you are limited to something that is too material and too rigid. Try and see structure as something more abstract, say, as a *network of relations*. For instance, think of the structure of our number system: when you name a number, you know where it belongs in the whole system, you know what

166

relations it has with any other number. The number 7 is always between the same neighbors, 6 and 8; it stands in a relation of 1 to 3 with 21, of 1 to 5 with 35; it is the square root of 49, the sum of 4 plus 3; it cannot be divided by 2 without breaking off one of its parts, and so on. Therefore, we say that numbers form a structure that holds together; they are ranked in order, they stand in definite relations to one another. If you use this structural order to classify things, for instance, if you number the books of your library according to the Dewey decimal system, you know where to look for any one of them.

Let us go one step further and make this notion of structure less rigid still. A musical score is the static presentation of a dynamic structure. It has a great many elements (notes) that run up and down a scale, appear and disappear at definite times, obey the pulsations of a definite rhythm, vary in intensity and color, and blend together in an overall effect. I remember one Saturday morning at Tanglewood, a few years ago, when De Sabata conducted a rehearsal of Beethoven's *Fifth Symphony*. He had the orchestra repeat a certain passage eleven times. At the sixth or seventh repetition, I felt that the results were as good as anybody could expect. But De Sabata kept on, pointing his baton in one direction, waving his hand in another, now whispering a remark, now singing softly a melodic design, urging with the harmonious tenseness of his whole body, living, as it were, the structure he wanted to recreate. Then the resounding masterpiece, made alive as if by magic, filled the air with waves of beauty that went through us all, deep into the silence of our admiration. In this sense, all human experiences can be described as structures, as conscious participations in a world of ordered processes.

But structures are not all of the same degree of complexity. Some are simple, like the melody of a flute; some are multiform and massive, like the full blast of a Wagner chorus. Some can be visualized, drawn on a piece of paper; some are too complex to be seen with the eye, and have to be felt by the whole organism to be really appreciated. There is no common measure for simple and complex structures. When we pass from one degree of complexity to another, we have to take what I call a "semantic jump" from one order of existence to another.

We often take such jumps. Like Monsieur Jourdain of Molière's comedy, who had been talking prose all his life and never knew it till his professor told him, we have been jumping from one semantic level to another without knowing it. But learning grammar and composition improves our prose, and being aware of where and how to take these semantic jumps does help, as we shall see.

This brings me to "dimensions" and "dimensionality." By dimension, I mean anything that can be measured, counted, evaluated, or described as more or less. In high-school geometry, space is described as having three dimensions at right angles with one another: length, width, and height. The surface of a mirror is said to be two-dimensional. A line has one dimension, and a point has no dimension at all.

Well, the terms "dimension" and "dimensionality" could be dematerialized even more, and brought to a higher order of abstraction. The letters that we use to make words can be taken as of a low order of dimensionality. We put them together, and depending on the order in which we place them, they assume a new dimensionality. For instance, with the three letters, D, G, O, I can have the structure DOG or the structure GOD, or four other structures, meaningless in our language: DGO, GDO, ODG, and OGD.

From words, we pass to sentences, and the rules of syntax guide us in giving them a meaningful structure. For instance, "The monkey threw a coconut at the bishop" makes sense; "The bishop threw a coconut at the monkey" remains a possibility; but "A coconut threw the bishop at the monkey" does not seem to make sense at all. We are now at a higher degree of dimensionality.

From sentences, we may pass to paragraphs, to chapters, to books, to a whole library on a particular subject, to the Library of Congress, if you wish. At each step, we pass to a higher order of objective abstraction, to a different level of dimensionality, through a range of structures that are not comparable to one another.

In music, we may go from single notes to melodies, to chords and counterpoint, to orchestration, and so on. In drawing, we have dots, lines, diagrams, and perspective projections. In pictures, we have still pictures, motion pictures, sound movies, colored sound movies, and cinerama. In all cases, each step involves new dimensions, different structures, and specific techniques. From one to the other we make what I call a "semantic jump." If we fail to do so, we confuse orders of existence, we flatten our world to a dull two-dimensional and very primitive picture, devoid of movement. We often do worse: since our language is forcedly linear, we may even reduce unwittingly the flowering richness of an experience to a series of words or ideas strung along the thread of what we call consistent logic.

I read about a good example of semantic jump in a simple experiment foisted upon his unsuspecting colleagues by Professor K. S. Lashley at the Hixon Symposium in 1948, and reported in the book, *Cerebral Mechanisms in Behavior*.[1] Lashley

---

[1] Lloyd A. Jeffress (ed.) *Cerebral Mechanisms in Behavior*, John Wiley and Sons, 1951, pp. 119–120.

had spoken of the cerebral mechanisms involved in the slips that often occur in writing and speaking, such as "Our queer old dean" for "Our dear old queen," or the typing of "wrapid writing" for "rapid writing," where the letter w is carried by anticipation from the second word to the first. Then he read aloud the following sentence, "Rapid righting with his uninjured hand saved from loss the contents of the capsized canoe." The audience all heard, "Rapid writing with his uninjured hand . . ." "Capsized canoe" required a complete and amusing about-face. The associations that were necessary to restructure the scene and give the contextual meaning to the word "righting" took three to five seconds to be activated. The linear series of words had put the audience on the wrong track.

We listen to people, and we run ahead of them, completing what we think they are going to express. Or we form an opinion from the first sentences of a paragraph before the author had time to build before us the multidimensional structure of his thoughts. Or we remain stubbornly at our preferred level, while the speaker is busy on some other level, a few orders higher or lower than our own.

Semantic motility is necessary. We must "keep on the jump."

CHAPTER XXVII

The Art of Semantic Jumping

✳ The other day I was describing to my friend Derm one of my pet notions: *me-and-my-world* forming a working unit that holds together, *me-and-my-world* as the only world that I know, that I live in, that came into existence when I was born, that will disappear when I die. He listened attentively and patiently. Then he said: "I understand what you say; each statement is quite acceptable to me. But the whole thing does not click with me. I don't get it, as I got other key notions that we have studied together."

Let us examine closely what happened. Derm is a very intelligent chap, highly cultured, open-minded, and interested in my explorations. He knows from experience that some of the notions we have studied together have suddenly glowed inside him, shooting out beams of insight in all directions, and transforming his outlook on himself and on the world in a spectacular fashion. This time, it does not work that way at all. He is ready to accept separately the various statements that I string out one after the other. Some may be weaker than others, of course, but none is rejected outright. However, he feels distinctly that these statements describe aspects of a semantic structure that apparently mean very much to me, while they fail to take shape within himself. The elements do not click together. He understands what I say, but does not get what I mean. He sees that I am all taken up with some notion that I cherish, but it leaves him cold.

This is an example of what I am trying to bring to light when I speak of a semantic jump. "What does the jumping?" you may ask with good reasons. "Well, I really don't know," I shall answer. You see, I am using an analogy here. In imagination, I "see" the molecules of a saturated solution jumping into place to form a recognizable crystal; I see the studdings, the boards and the nails that the carpenters put together to build a shed next door; I see the light of the sun, the water and the soil chemicals that the potted geranium puts silently together to form its leaves and its flowers on the window sill; I hear the separate instrumental themes that De Sabata brought together into a harmonious whole at the Tanglewood rehearsal; I feel the chaotic bits of personal knowledges and experiences that occasionally fit together within me and give me a thrilling insight. I call this a "jump," to emphasize the suddenness, the newness, and the "renewal-ness" of the whole experience. It gives me the impression of passing from one stage of living to a different one. If you ask me, "Is it your 'ideas' that come together and assume a new structure, or is it yourself who undergo a change in your attitudes?" I confess that I cannot answer in an either-or way. It is something that happens somewhere within what I call my semantic reactions, and I describe it as a "jump," for want of a better term. Sometimes it is a slow jump, sometimes it is a quick jump. When I become aware of it, it is a personal discovery and a fresh start.

If we refer to the semantic reaction diagram (page 44), we see that these jumps can be brought about by a change in any of the five areas described there: thinking, feeling, self-moving, electrochemical, and environmental. A change of scene makes you feel different; the surge of gonadic hormones makes the child an adolescent; gardening with your own hands is not like looking at flowers; falling in love makes you see people differently; accepting a theory may give a new orientation to your whole life.

We are familiar with Shakespeare's "All the world's a stage," in which he brings before us the seven parts that man plays from the cradle to the grave: the infant, "mewling and puking"; the schoolboy, "creeping like snail unwillingly to school"; the lover, "sighing like furnace"; the soldier, "full of strange oaths, sudden and quick in quarrels"; the justice, "with fair round belly, full of wise saws"; the "lean and slipper'd pantaloon, with spectacles on nose"; and the "second childishness and oblivion, sans teeth, sans eyes, sans taste, sans everything." From one act to the other, what a change in the actor and in his world!

When people fail to take the jump from one role to the next, we speak of "regression to the infantile stage," of "immaturity," of "failure to develop," of "not keeping up with the times!" Psychotherapy is concerned with semantic jumps, with people who failed to jump out of childish dependency, with people who jump too far ahead in anxious expectation. In business, I remember the case of Mac, who failed to jump from being a "shop boss" to being a factory manager. He had done extremely well, twenty years ago, when the business was a small shop with a dozen employees. When the place became a plant, with three hundred workers on a production line, he did not jump out of his "small shop world" and had to be removed, shop and all, into services and repair.

You know people whose married life is the legalized concubinage of two chance acquaintances; they did not take the jump from bachelorhood into a life-of-two-for-two. You know the accounting expert who became general manager but who persists in seeing everything within the narrow columns of financial control. You know the wife of the climbing executive who remains the small-town girl that he met when he was a small-town boy. You know the old man who keeps reminiscing about the past because he has not the vigor to jump forward, nor the stamina to withstand the jolts of the present.

This jump is a leap into the unknown, into an order of existence that was not before, that cannot be foreseen in all its aspects, that often demands a readaptation of our thoughts, feelings, and habits in more ways than we can anticipate. There is no point-to-point correspondence between the situation before the jump and the situation after the jump; they cannot be described in the same terms; they have no common measure. They belong to two different orders of dimensionality, like the circle and the sphere, the square and the cube. If we translate the higher order into terms of the lower, we distort it; we destroy the very difference that makes it different; we deny the experience that goes with it.

The semantic jump is by nature an irreversible process that we make reversible at a cost to ourselves.

More than once, I have seen lives that have been crippled because of such an unwitting reversal. Here is a man who seems to cling desperately to a theory of life, religious or philosophical, that tears him apart. He fights against himself in contradictions that he can neither overcome nor pacify. If I try to argue with him, he will pass from one theory to another with a clever swiftness that leaves me panting. What's wrong?

I suspect that there is somewhere in his past an experience, a semantic jump into the unknown that he has not assimilated, not rationalized. Because this experience is not translated into accepted terms, he has denied it; but it remains within him as a source of energies that he cannot hold in check. The new self that the experience has created is threatening to destroy the old self that fights for dear life; his world is tottering, it will bury him under its ruins. He is panicky, terrified, desperate. He is trying to reverse the irreversible; he is in distress and will fight whoever approaches him.

In the case that I have in mind as I write this, the man had gone through an experience of felt oneness with nature that corresponds to stage 5 of the epistemological profile given in chapters XVI and XVII. For a short entrancing moment he had lived in a world devoid of classifications, formulas, and postulates. He could not deny this experience, but, being unable to rationalize it to himself or to explain it to others, he had put it aside as irrelevant, mysterious, or foolishly sentimental.

Once he accepted it as a normal human experience and learned to appreciate its value, he regained his interior peace.

He is now trying to move into this new world the elements of his past experiences, theories, and habits that can be carried over the semantic jump.

Life is a succession of leaps into the unknown. As the unknown becomes known, my knowledge makes a multiordinal jump that multiplies the dimensions of the world in which I live. The art of living may be called the art of semantic jumping.

CHAPTER XXVIII

Our Space-Time World

✳ The first time I read that Einstein wanted us to adopt a "new way of thinking," I took it as one of those pieces of good advice that scientists give us occasionally, and, to tell you the truth, it left me cold. Then, I began wondering about what they meant by the "fourth dimension" and by a "space-time world." Later on, I read that space and time were nothing but ideas in our heads, "mental constructs" as they call them. It became more and more evident to me that this new way of thinking must be related to these unusual notions. I had to take a jump into a new kind of semantic reaction, different from what I was accustomed to. In this chapter, I shall describe my semantic jump as best I can. To tell you the whole story would take a volume, and you cannot be interested in the very personal incidents of my explorations. I shall limit myself to a few turning points of the road I blazed through the Unknown.

My knowledge of mathematics is limited to the first stages of calculus. So, I knew that I could not take the royal road to my objective. I read a few "popular" books on the subject, such as Gamow's *One, Two, Three . . . Infinity*, the very attractive and stimulating booklets of the Liebers, starting with *The Education of T. C. Mits*, but I could not go very far on this main highway. The grades were too steep and too twisting for me. I got dizzy on the heights. You see, I belong to the generation whose school education was of the Model T type: there were no such highways and no such powerful cars in those days. The high-school graduate of today is probably more at home in the world of mathematics than I am. The main thing that I learned from my attempts was that there is no common measure to these two semantic worlds, the four-dimensional that I wanted to enter and the three-dimensional in which I had learned to live. If I were to jump from one to the other, I would have to do it by playing some trick on my own perceptions.

The Ames experiments gave me a clue. By this time you must know of the Ames experiments. If not, read about them in the books on the subject listed in the bibliography, or, better still, go and see those that may be available in your part of the country.

Well, one of the things that I got from these experiments is that *perspective has taught us to perceive a third dimension where there are only two.* Perspective was surely a great discovery for the painters of the Renaissance: it gave depth to a flat canvas. Distorting a rectangle into a trapezoid liberated them from mental constructs that were not true to life and gave them a means of seeing what was not there! The art of man caught up with nature's illusions: in the square pane of glass that faces me at my desk, I "see" my neighbor's house behind a tree, without having to go behind the tree to see it. In Macy's restaurant, the mirror that covers the wall in the back gives me a feeling of space, depth, and light, that extends way beyond the wall itself.

Now, let us transpose this experience one step higher. If we have learned to see depth where there is no depth, to perceive a third dimension on a flat canvas, is it possible to get the feel of a fourth dimension in a three-dimensional diagram? Is it possible to blend time with space and obtain a genuine semantic reaction to *space-time?* I think it is.

Let us come back to the semantic-reaction diagram, which we can now draw a bit differently to give us a picture of man on the time dimension, as in the accompanying figure. From birth till death, our life can be seen as a series of semantic

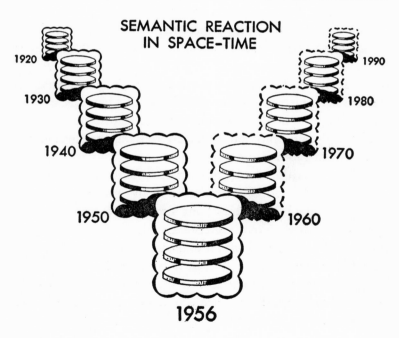

SEMANTIC REACTION
IN SPACE-TIME

1920

1930

1940

1950

1956

1960

1970

1980

1990

reactions, of perceived and acted fittings to an environment that changes ceaselessly. In the center of the figure, we have a semantic reaction diagram drawn in heavier lines. It is a "still" picture of the *now*, of what happens in this operational unit or system, which we may call "me-and-my-world-at-a-definite-moment." The question is: "Are the 'past' and the 'future' present in the 'now'?" The answer is: "Yes, they are." They operate in the "now" with their relative intensity, their direction, and their tensions. I am now the living cumulative result of my past and the active sum total of my future, anticipated consciously or unconsciously. When you touch me by a statement, a gesture, a handshake, a kick, or a kiss, you establish a contact with a space-time living totality that reacts with everything that it has been, is, and anticipates being.

Don't look at the early experiences of your childhood as things of the past. "Past" is only a way of speaking. It is just as true, even truer, to speak about them differently and say, "They are here now, they operate here now, they influence my reactions at this moment, right here." I do not have to dig into my unconscious to find the fossils of my early experiences and reanimate them by reliving their emotions; I simply have to become aware of what is right here, striving and pressing within me at this very moment.

My future is here and now as well, my future as I anticipate it, confusedly perhaps; my future as a growing adolescent who dreams of a mate, as an adult who wants to get ahead in his profession, as an older man who sees the sun of his world going down in golden light. All this is here, now, throbbing, pulsating, acting in a space-time plenum that is more real than what I am accustomed to see, to speak of, to theorize about.

The here-now, represented by the semantic reaction frame in the center and marked 1956, is a living mirror facing both the past and the future, receiving and projecting the living thoughts, feelings, habits, and electrochemical activities of a space-time organism that stands as the energy center of my world, as the nuclear core of my atom that spins autono- mously in the cosmic vortex.

All these words that pour out of my pencil are faint pic- tures of pale analogies, I know. If you take them one by one, you may find their standard meaning in your vocabulary or in the dictionary. But the meaning of my message is not in them. They are elements of a living structure that I cannot communicate to you as I feel it. Look at this apple tree, right here in the garden, on this spring day. Its past is there, from the days when it was planted, grafted, nurtured and sprayed; its winter sleep is there; its awakening stares you in the face; its blossoms are bursting to come out to the sun; its fruits are calling for the sap to run up and fill them with its juice. The tree in space-time is the "real" tree. To be aware of what is going on, I must take a semantic jump be- yond appearances and "realize" it, make it become real for me.

With a bit of training you will see the whole world in this way. Here is an institution, a business enterprise, a church, a university, or a foundation. We say that it has a history and a purpose. Bring that past and that future into the now, and see them operating as active forces right under your eyes. Don't expect to change them overnight, or in a year or two. "Overnight," "a year or two," are "time" notions, mere constructs of your own mind. They are abstractions from a process that follows the course of its own integrity. That process has energetic nuclear cores, men, like you and me.

Some are like the steadfast nuclei of unfissionable material. At the present stage of our knowledge, they won't change unless destroyed. Some are nearer the point of tremendous energy release: they are the radioactive elements of humankind. The search for the philosopher's stone has brought us to a space-time material world where atomic fission is possible; we have to learn to live in a space-time world of human beings if we want to achieve the age-long dream of the seers and change human nature.

CHAPTER XXIX

Guided Awareness

✳ "Are you listening to yourself as you talk to me?" I asked Fred.

He was bewildered by such a question. "What do you mean?" he said. "I don't have to listen to myself. I know very well what I want to say. It's you who are supposed to do the listening, not me!"

He kept on. He is a fast and voluble speaker, logical, never at a loss for the telling word, hammering in punch line after punch line. He saw that I was not impressed. He brought into action his heaviest artillery, exhausted his ammunition, and eventually came to a stop. Then he looked at me quizzically. "You old devil," he said, "what is that trick you are up to? Why do you want me to listen to what I say when you don't listen yourself?"

"Fred," I said, "I was listening both to what you said and

to the manner in which you said it. Your manner destroyed your message as you went along."

Yes, there is the manner and there is the talk. There is the manner in which we speak, and, more important still, there is the manner in which we talk to ourselves when we do some "thinking." To listen to ourselves while thinking, to observe and manage our semantic reactions as they stir and shift through our total organism, is one of the most demanding tasks that I know. It calls for the skill of *guided awareness.*

In recent years, there has been a great deal of research in communication, automatic controls, and neurology. From this research, the notion of "feedback" has become a common one. Feedback mechanisms are devices that watch and control performance. They answer the questions: "How am I doing? When shall I stop, start again, change course?" They set off actions and reactions.

The thermostat on the wall watches the temperature of the room and starts the furnace when necessary. A device in the nose of a guided missile watches a shifting objective and directs the mechanism that steers the weapon. Your wife gives you feedback when she kicks you under the bridge table when you fail to trump your opponent's trick. The orchestra leader watches the musicians and the score and regulates the performance.

There are thousands of feedback mechanisms in our own body. For every nerve fiber carrying a message from our brain to some part of our body, there is a returning one that reports on how the job is being done. Feedback mechanisms keep the temperature of our blood to about 98.6° Fahrenheit. Some control the rate of our breathing; some keep our endocrine glands in balance. Some are acquired, such as the way we write, speak, walk, and drive our car. Some are unconscious, some are partly conscious. Habits can be described as feedback mechanisms that we have grafted to our organism. In a sense, language is one in that most of our thinking movements are limited to what our language allows. We miss what it does not encompass; we follow blindly the thinking sequences that it sets into action.

In most feedback mechanisms, there is a control unit that receives the messages from the operating system and sends out the orders that direct the ensuing performance. The pituitary gland in the body and the thermostat are examples. How shall we provide a control unit that receives the messages coming from the various parts of that space-time operating system that we pictured in the semantic-reaction diagram of the previous chapter (page 179)?

I suggest an "awareness unit," a center of cultivated sensitivity to the phenomena, clues, and indications that we have studied so far. I see this awareness as different from morbid introspection. It does not ask itself, "*Why* am I this way or that way? *Why* do I feel as I do?" but it checks on the observable "what-I-say," "what-I-do," on the muscular tensions and movements that are within my control, on the sensations that I can register and observe. These will provide me with many indicators that reveal the condition of my semantic balance and give me the choice of an appropriate course of remedial action. This awareness unit would be like the clinical thermometer that reveals the presence of an infection, the blood-pressure manometer that tells the strength of the heart, the glucose tolerance test that detects overproduction of insulin.

As progress is made in the science of man, more and more indicators come within the range of our awareness. Some are detected and measured with scientific instruments and techniques and we cannot be concerned with them here. We shall leave them to the specialists: the neurologist with his E.E.G., the psychologist with his ink blots, the pathologist with his test tubes. But there are many more than we suspect that can be observed by the layman who wants to know himself and to manage himself. If we learn to pay attention to them, we shall: 1) stop wearing ourselves out or destroying ourselves by excessive bursts of energy; 2) keep functioning within an optimum range of efficiency; 3) adapt ourselves to shifting objectives and changing conditions.

These indicators are within the observable range of *what we say, what we do, how we say it,* and *how we do it.* They can be measured roughly on a qualitative scale from *danger signs* to *safety signs.* Here are a few of them. The danger indicators are in roman type; the corresponding safety indicators are in italics:

We use absolute terms, generalities, abstractions of a
high order, words that imply
"allness,"

                    or

            we use descriptive terms and lower
            order abstractions, statements as to
            who, what, where, when, and
            how much.

We use judgment terms,
terms loaded with approval
or disapproval,

                    or

            we use neutral terms, terms that
            are as free as possible from bias or
            slant.

We use "either-or" arguments, pass from one alternative to its extreme opposite, describe things in terms of black and white without any gray shading in between,

or

we speak in terms of more-or-less, give consideration to degrees and shades of meaning, avoid talking about opposites.

We speak of the present situation as "just like" another one, of this person as "just like" So-and-so, of this problem as "just like" the one solved previously,

or

we differentiate carefully between people, situations, and problems.

We confuse facts that can be verified by anybody, and interpretations, opinions, and judgments that are exclusively our own,

or

we distinguish between what is going on and what we feel or understand is going on.

We ramble from one subject to another,

or

we keep to the subject under discussion.

We quote authorities to up-
hold our viewpoint,

or

we try to evaluate the situation on its own merits.

We quibble on the dictionary
meaning of words,

or

we use words as mere tokens for what we wish to convey.

We talk fast and/or loud,

or

we talk with deliberation.

We interrupt, start talking before the other fellow is finished, we contradict with a
quick "yes/but,"

or

we listen with genuine attention, wait for our turn to speak, begin with something like "If this is what you mean, then . . ."

We keep muscles tense, move
in jerks, fidget, twitch,

or

we relax, remain calm and quiet, and delay our reactions.

We ask rhetorical and tricky
questions,

or

*we ask matter-of-fact questions
that invite more information.*

We get flushed, we grow pale,
we screw our face in knots,

or

*we breathe evenly, we keep an
emerging smile, we keep our
composure.*

"This is old stuff," you may say. "This is just a code of
gentlemanly behavior presented as a scientific scheme."

Please, wait a minute! Delay your reactions and look well!
Yes, there is some "old stuff" in this, in the sense that much
of it has been preached by moralists and by teachers of good
manners. But there is a good deal of "new stuff" too.

First, these indicators are not presented here as a list of rules
that you must follow; they are given as indicators of smooth
functioning that you can check occasionally, as you watch
the dials and the lights on the control panel of your car.
They reveal how things are going on inside of you—"under
the hood," to continue the analogy—and it is left entirely
to you to heed the signals or to take a chance.

Second, they are not given as *laws from above* but as *laws
from inside*. Laws from above (in French, "lois de notre
maître") are imposed upon us by some outside authority;
laws from inside (in French, "lois de notre être") are described by scientists as the internal requirements of a system
in operation. We have them in chemical formulas, in physical and biological laws. We are theoretically free to ignore
them, but if we do, something is bound to go wrong.

Third, they can be checked by experiment, as any natural
law can be checked. Give them a try and see what happens.

I have tried them in a variety of situations, with myself, with individuals who came for counseling, with business groups for which I acted as moderator. For instance, listen to the tape recording of any discussion, in business or elsewhere. You will notice that statements often overlap at the ends: Jack has not quite finished speaking when Bill starts with his own bit of wisdom, which he cannot give in full before Harry cuts in. Misunderstandings occur, confusion grows apace, the chairman has to intervene, or the matter is passed on to a subcommittee. Instead of this, try the safety rule, "Wait for your turn to speak," and ask each discusser to wait until at least one second has elapsed after the other fellow has shut his mouth before opening his own. You will be amazed at the results. And it is good clean fun, too.

Fourth, these indicators are so closely related that by paying attention to one you correct almost automatically the malfunctioning revealed by the others. You will see that the organism works as a whole, that body and mind interact. Just relax until you feel the seat of your pants, and you will notice that your tendency to generalize or to quibble about words subsides noticeably. Slow down your talking speed, and you will think more clearly. Listen to yourself as you speak, and you will suddenly realize why the other fellow is not impressed.

If you want a name for the type of behavior that I suggest, you may call it "C-behavior." It is a behavior guided by a fuller *consciousness* of what is going on inside ourselves and in the environment; it involves a reflexive use of our thinking activities (area C of the semantic-reaction diagram).

Self-training in C-behavior takes time, patience, and persistence.

First you have to learn to recognize the danger and safety

indicators quickly and accurately. This is not as simple as it sounds. In a heated discussion with others or in a conflicting situation within ourselves, it is practically impossible to recognize them and to heed them. I have found that it is easier to begin by studying a letter, a memorandum, or an article, and to pick as many high-order abstractions, absolute terms, and judgment terms as I can recognize. Next, you may analyze a few tape recordings of discussions or casual conversations in which you took part. This will give you a wider range of indicators to observe. The indicators at the body level, such as tension, fast speech, non-listening, and the like, are easier to detect. If you feel like it, ask a friend to point them out to you.

Next you must practice your new skills. Practice one or no more than two or three at a time. Choose the one that is easiest for you to recognize and to control. Make your choice by trying a few of them, just to see what happens. For instance, a bit of physical relaxation right in the course of a tough interview may achieve unexpected results; a careful use of neutral terms, of low-order descriptive words may take the heat out of a discussion; a delayed reaction with a smile may relieve interpersonal tension; a question that is not tricky but genuinely asks for information may give the argument a different direction.

Lastly, you must keep practicing until C-behavior becomes a habit that functions almost by itself, like driving your car. When you reach this stage, you will feel uncomfortable when your semantic reactions get out of the optimum range for a while, just as you feel vaguely from your steering that a tire is going flat. Remedial action will then be easy and effective.

You will notice that practice and knowledge stimulate each other—the more you practice, the better you under-

stand; the better you understand, the more skilled you become. The art of C-behavior is like any other art; it involves
study and action. It becomes more interesting and more
exciting as you become more sensitive to its fine points and
more expert in performance.

"Will this program make life stilted and dull?" you may
ask. Well, it may, if you take it too much in earnest, if you
are "obsessive-compulsive" about it, as the psychiatrists
would say.

This brings me to a final pair of danger-safety indicators
that sum up the whole program for us.

We take ourselves very seri-
ously,

or

we keep our sense of humor.

CHAPTER XXX

The Lifting Power

✳ It was a clear morning in January. From the top of the hill where we stood, we saw the village spread irregularly on the snow blanket, the farmhouses here and there on the edges, the village buildings crowded together at the crossroads where the church stood with its pointed steeple. From every chimney a white mushroom of smoke was going up straight, floating steadily in the cold air.

"Wouldn't it be fun if we could walk on smoke with our snowshoes?" said Johanna, then eight years old, who was enjoying for the first time the glorious sensation of tramping on the fluffy snow.

For a child, smoke floats in the air. If you had enough of it, well-packed and spread about, you could walk on it with snowshoes, couldn't you?

The Montgolfier brothers were not any wiser than Johanna when they got the idea of their "aerostatic globes" and invented the balloon. They, too, thought that smoke floats in the air. They guessed that, if they could harness billows of smoke in a huge bag, the lightness—the "levity" as they called it—would buoy up the whole contraption above the roof-tops. They tried it, and it worked. But their theory was all wrong: it was not the visible smoke that lifted the balloon; it was the invisible heat that did the work.

When we observe the ascent of Smith from his Stone Age primitiveness to his culture of today, we make a similar mistake. We explain his progress by what we can see: his inventions, his monuments, and his writings. We see geniuses as stage-rockets at each burst of advance; we reprint the Great Books and we urge people to assimilate their wisdom; we look upon knowledge as the driving force that brings us up to dizzy heights.

Knowledge is like the smoke of the Montgolfiers' balloon. Unless it contains with its solid particles the lifting energy of human warmth, it has no ascending power. Geniuses have made the world better in the measure that they have loved men. The form of energy that has lifted man above himself may appear to be mind-energy, but a more discriminative science begins to realize that the motive power is different. Today you begin to read in scientific literature about love-energy and its measurement. Mind-energy is the billowing smoke that you see; love-energy is the powerful drive that comes from a burning heart.

We are still a bit shy about speaking freely of love-energy. We would rather speak of "morale," of "team work," of "tolerance," of "togetherness," of "good-neighbor policies," of "affiliative tendencies," of "a need for belongingness," of the "spirit of Geneva."

It was years ago that Cassius J. Keyser wrote the cryptic

statement, "To be is to be related." This is acceptable. It is like the conclusion of a theorem that you cannot escape once you accept the premises. Korzybski expands this viewpoint when he asserts that Smith is not only a chemistry-binder like plants, or a space-binder like animals, but time-bound and time-binding, from the emergence of homo sapiens to the farthest reaches of the future he can picture to himself.

The moralists and the religious teachers were for a long time the only people to deal with this subject. In our Western culture we have the immortal Chapter 13 of 1 Corinthians, in which St. Paul describes "agape," the conscious acceptance of felt togetherness.

Are these statements of St. Paul, Korzybski, Keyser and of a host of others just empty theories? Is the commandment "Love thy neighbor as thyself" an arbitrary dictate of the God of Jewish-Christian tradition? Is the "Sermon on the Mount" a lofty code of behavior proposed to a limited number of self-sacrificing volunteers?

The cold, experimental, and pedestrian science of our day is gradually formulating an answer to these questions. The answer is that *altruism is not a matter of choice; it belongs to the nature of man.* The consequence is that the skill to love creatively is as important as, if not more important than, the skill to think creatively.

Look for this answer in such books as Ashley Montague's recent book, *The Direction of Human Development*, in Trigant Burrow's experimental reports and learned discussions on phylobiology, in the 1956 best-seller *Love or Perish* by Smiley Blanton, in *Love Against Hate* by Karl Menninger. Harvard University has a Research Center in Altruistic Integration and Creativity—what a mouthful!—under the direction of

Pitirim A. Sorokin, "whose purpose," states its director, "is to study love in its various aspects, and especially to explore efficient ways of producing, accumulating, and circulating love-energy in the human universe."[1] Elsewhere the same social scientist writes: "Even from a purely utilitarian and hedonistic standpoint, these verities are so significant that an intensive study of love—of its how and why, of the techniques of its 'production,' 'accumulation,' and 'circulation'— can no longer be neglected if humanity wants to survive and to continue its creative mission."[2]

The day may not be far distant when we shall attach as much importance to the love quotient as we do now to the intelligence quotient. We already evaluate the four doctorates of Albert Schweitzer as less significant than his self-sacrificing devotedness to his patients at Lambaréné. Great love dynamos, like Gandhi, Francis of Assisi, and Jesus, may be seen as superior to the religious and political engineers who have confined to narrow channels the powerful energies that surged from their hearts. Forgiving fathers and loving mothers may eventually be recognized as equally necessary as human-relations experts and group therapists.

Once a business man, who had studied with me some of the notions developed here and a few others of the same type, came out with the following remarks: "Doctor, you gave us an impressive display of experiments, exercises, and discussions, all in the name of the most up-to-date science. It sounded so 'scientific' that, for a while, I was overwhelmed. But now, when I sum it all up in my own mind, it becomes very simple. All you did is to show us that in business as

---

[1] Pitirim A. Sorokin, *Explorations in Altruistic Love and Behavior*, The Beacon Press, 1950, p. vi.

[2] Pitirim A. Sorokin, *Altruistic Love*, The Beacon Press, 1950, p. vi.

elsewhere there are two virtues that it pays to practice. They used to be called 'humility' and 'charity.' You streamlined them and gave them new names, that's about all."

Well, I leave it to you to judge the validity of his remarks. According to Poincaré, "All the scientist creates in a fact is the language in which he enunciates it." On the other hand, "A language of new structure has a kind of creative character, in that it makes some structural discoveries easier."[3]

The old word "humility, implies too often submission and subservience. To me, this is not a healthy word any more. If you replace it with "awareness of your limitations," you recognize that none of your thoughts and none of your utterances are adequate. You stop being so decidedly positive in what you say, but you do not lose a bit of self-respect for all that.

"Charity" has not fared much better. It is connected with "almsgiving," with pity for those in need, with a feeling of praiseworthy munificence in the giver. In fact, the original text of St. Paul used another word, "agape," which has no equivalent in English. "Agape" could be described as a conscious acceptance and a thorough understanding of our relatedness to all other human beings. It is wrapped in a genuine tenderness of feeling towards them. It is related to loving our neighbor as we actually love ourselves.

With due respect for St. Paul, I give here my own translation in today's language of his well-known chapter on agape.

Though I speak with the language of religious men or common men, and have not agape, I am like an empty container.

And though I have predictability, and understand higher mathematics and other forms of representation, and though I have

[3] Korzybski, *Science and Sanity*, p. 242.

scientific knowledge that can blast away mountains, and do not have agape, I am as nothing.

And though I support organized charity and risk my life for worthy causes, this will be of no value, have I not agape.

Agape accepts the world of human beings, and is kind; agape does not envy, it does not boast; it does not behave inappropriately, it does not seek personal advantage, it is not easily provoked, nor is it defensive.

Agape thrives not on graft, or injustice, but rejoices in knowledge of what is fair.

Agape withstands the pressure of anxiety, has faith in the goodness of human nature, hopes for better things, endures through changes.

Agape never fails, but predictability may fail, and languages and other forms of representation may fail—graphs, charts, formulae—these all may fail. For we know only in part. As yet we have only peepholes into reality. We can predict only in part. There are always characteristics left out. There is always the et cetera.

And when we know more, that which we knew in part will be called obsolete, and will be cast aside, or revised.

When I was a child, I behaved and evaluated as a child; now that I am an adult, I try to behave and evaluate as an adult, and to put away childish ways.

And now we see through our hidden assumptions, our prejudices, our stereotypes, our past judgments; we live in our isolated individual worlds; but as we know our own limitations, we grow beyond them.

And now we reduce this to faith in scientific methods, hope in man's growth by their use, and love of everyone in conscious agape, which excels above all else.

CHAPTER XXXI

Between You and Me

✳ You and I have gone together for many pages, exploring our individual world, each of us in our own way. I did all the talking. You probably did some too, but I did not hear you. Such are the shortcomings of written communication.

Before taking leave, I would like to tell you what prompted me to write, and what prompts me to stop at this point.

I see our times as the age of the common man. I was not just talking when I wrote: "We are conscious that what we think, feel, say, and do, has a creative or distorting influence on the world we shall live in at the next moment, tomorrow, and for years" (page 88). I meant something that is fundamental in my philosophy of life.

I, as a common man, need no anointing from any priesthood of science or philosophy to exert some influence around

199

me. Nobody does. Whether we realize it or not, we influence our space-time environment, and we are influenced by it. I don't know what you did today or yesterday; I don't know your age, your occupation, nor your family life. But, if you review what happened, you will discover many things that were so because you made them so. Jean-Paul Sartre has this to say about the creative power of words alone: "The serious error . . . is to think that the word is a gentle breeze which plays lightly over the surface of things, which grazes them without altering them, and that the speaker is a pure *witness* who sums up with a word his harmless contemplation. To speak is to act; anything which one names is already no longer the same; it has lost its innocence."[1]

So, the common man, the plain Smith like me, should be aware of the possible effects of what he says when he writes to people he does not even know. By coming in print, I knocked at the door of your life. You let me in and you listened to me. I feel that between the two of us a personal relationship has been established. I didn't write for the "public"; I wrote for each individual Smith who is willing to read a long personal letter from an unknown relative, from another Smith of his day and age.

When I graduated from college—that was before World War I—I saw around me a world that has changed a great deal since. Politically, it looked like a fairly stable world. There were kings and emperors in large numbers, colonies that didn't seem to mind being colonies, a white Western supremacy that went unchallenged. World government was not mentioned that I remember. We had to have a first World War to try a League of Nations, and a second one in order to start all over again with the United Nations. Russia

[1] Whit Burnett (ed.), *The World's Best*, The Dial Press, 1950, p. 727.

did not count very much then, and the United States kept itself securely locked within the walls of the Monroe Doctrine. China was China, period. India was within the British Empire, upon which the sun never set. Things are so different today that I can hardly recreate in my memory a vivid picture of what they were then.

Our universities were colleges with a few professional schools that often enjoyed a relative independence. Graduate work was just beginning. Science was at peace with itself. The disturbers of this peace, Einstein, Poincaré, Planck, Freud, and the rest of them, were a minority and a curiosity. We were then refining our measurements of the world we had conquered; we never expected it to blow up into unpredictable dimensions right in our face.

I need not say much of the technological and industrial changes that have taken place. At that time, there was no rumbling of trucks on the roads, no jet planes in the air, no diesels on the rails, no television in the homes, no nylon stockings, no deep-freezes, no plastics, no super markets, no mechanical bookkeeping, no electronic brains.

When people advanced in age beyond the fifties, they were old people. None but the very sturdy exceptions ventured beyond the "three score and ten" of the Bible. There were no vitamins, no hormones, and no antibiotics to keep one going in those days. The population has shifted since then: more people finish high school, a larger proportion go to college, the suburbanites have become a new social class, adult education is more generalized, magazines and pocket books popularize science from psychoanalysis to atomic fission, high-fidelity records bring symphonies into the home, radio and TV keep us in hour-to-hour contact with the far corners of the earth, with science-fiction we leap into space.

It is commonplace to say that we live in a world of change. It is common sense to adapt ourselves to change.

But it is not so easy. We yearn for absolutes; we look for steady indicators to fixate our bearings; we clamor for security. Psychiatry has popular appeal; religion fought it for a while and now joins forces with it. Books on positive thinking and peace of mind remain on the best-seller lists for years; physicists talk like philosophers, and philosophers emulate scientists; psychologists have put aside their brass instruments to probe into "affiliative tendencies" and to engineer human relations; management begins to realize that running a business calls for statesmanship of the highest type.

Our thinking is stirred almost to the point of confusion; our values are shifting. It reminds me of my first experience in an airplane, over twenty-five years ago. I had boarded the hydroplane that flew on the Genoa-Rome-Naples-Palermo run. We gained momentum in the small harbor of Ostia at right angles with our intended course along the Italian coast. We were no sooner airborne than the pilot banked his machine sharply to the left at an altitude of only a few hundred feet. The distant sea disappeared on the right, and the shore came up against the window on the left where I expected the horizon to be. Up was down, and down was up. I had lost my bearings in a world that I did not control.

Today we are used to smoother flying, with instruments that guide the awareness of the pilot beyond the limits of his sense perceptions. I am hoping for a similar awareness in human affairs by means of scientific methods applied to the piloting of our fast moving life. I do not ignore the cardinal points of the moral compass; I want better instruments to navigate speedily and safely in a world of many more dimensions than our forebears could anticipate. I do not propose any revolution in our thinking, in our institutions, or in our way of life; I simply want to make the most of what we already have and to do my limited share in casting aside or revising the obsolete methods that cramp our style. I offer no all-embracing system, no guaranteed panacea, no sure-firing bomb.

And I stop right here, because I know that whatever I say, I shall never finish saying what I want to say. You too have many things in your heart and mind. If I have stirred them up a bit, I am satisfied. You carry on from here.

Bibliography

Abbott, Edwin A. *Flatland*. New York: Dover Publications, 1952.

Allport, Floyd H. *Theories of Perception and the Concept of Structure*. New York: John Wiley and Sons, 1955.

Bachelard, Gaston, Schrödinger, Erwin, et al. *L'homme devant la science*. Neuchâtel, Switzerland: Editions de la Baconnière, 1953.

Bachelard, Gaston, *La Philosophie du Non*. Paris: Presses Universitaires de France, 1949.

Bartlett, F. C. *Remembering*. London: Cambridge University Press, 1932.

Benedict, Ruth. *The Chrysanthemum and the Sword*. Boston: Houghton Mifflin, 1946.

Beveridge, W. I. B. *The Art of Scientific Investigation*. London: William Heineman, Ltd., 1950.

Blake, Robert R., and Ramsey, Glenn V. (eds.). *Perception, An Approach to Personality*. New York: The Ronald Press, 1951.

Blanton, Smiley. *Love or Perish*. New York: Simon and Schuster, 1956.

Bornemisza, Stephen T. *The Unified System Concept of Nature*. New York: The Vantage Press, 1955.

Burrow, Trigant. *Science and Man's Behavior*. New York: Philosophical Library, 1953.

Bryson, Lyman, et al. (eds.). *Symbols and Society*. New York: Harper & Brothers, 1955.

Cantril, Hadley. *The "Why" of Human Experience*. New York: The Macmillan Company, 1950.

Chapin, Miriam. *How People Talk*. New York: The John Day Company, 1945.

Chase, Stuart. *Power of Words*. New York: Harcourt, Brace, 1953.

Chase, Stuart. *Roads to Agreement*. New York: Harper & Brothers, 1951.

Dewey, John, and Bentley, Arthur F. *Knowing and the Known*. Boston: The Beacon Press, 1949.

Dunne, J. W. *An Experiment with Time*. London: Faber & Faber, 1927.

Dunne, J. W. *The Serial Universe*. London: Faber & Faber, 1934.

Einstein, Albert. *Conceptions scientifiques, morales et sociales*. Paris: Flammarion, 1952.

Einstein, Albert. *Relativity, the Special and General Theory*. New York: Henry Holt, 1947.

Evans, Bergen. *The Natural History of Nonsense.* New York: Alfred A. Knopf, 1946.

Field, Sara Bard. *Collected Poems of Charles Erskine Scott Wood.* New York: The Vanguard Press, 1949.

Frank, Philipp. *Modern Science and Its Philosophy.* Cambridge: Harvard University Press, 1941.

Gamow, George. *One, two, three . . . infinity.* New York: The Viking Press, 1947.

Gibran, Kahlil. *The Prophet.* New York: Alfred A. Knopf, 1946.

Hayakawa, S. I. *Language in Thought and Action.* New York: Harcourt, Brace, 1949.

Hebb, D. O. *The Organization of Behavior.* New York: John Wiley & Sons, 1949.

Hogben, Lancelot. *Mathematics for the Million.* London: George Allen & Unwin, 1936.

Isherwood, Christopher (ed.). *Vedanta for Modern Man.* New York: Harper & Brothers, 1951.

Jeffress, Lloyd A. (ed.). *Cerebral Mechanisms in Behavior.* New York: Harper & Brothers, 1951.

Johnson, Wendell. *People in Quandaries.* New York: Harper & Brothers, 1946.

Kasner, Edward, and Newman, James. *Mathematics and the Imagination.* New York: Simon and Schuster, 1940.

Kelly, Earl C. *Education for What Is Real.* New York: Harper & Brothers, 1947.

Kendig, M. (ed.). *Papers from the Second American Congress of General Semantics.* Chicago: Institute of General Semantics, 1943.

Keyser, Cassius Jackson. *Mathematics as a Culture Clue.* New York: Scripta Mathematica, Yeshiva University, 1947.

Keyserling, Count Hermann. *South American Meditations.* New York: Harper & Brothers, 1932.

Kilpatrick, Franklin P. (ed.). *Human Behavior from the Transactional Point of View.* Hanover: Institute for Associated Research, 1951.

Kline, Morris. *Mathematics in Western Culture.* New York: Oxford University Press, 1953.

Kluckohn, Clyde. *Mirror for Man.* New York: McGraw-Hill, 1949.

Korzybski, Alfred. *Manhood of Humanity,* 2nd ed., International Non-Aristotelian Library Publishing Company, 1950.

Korzybski, Alfred. *Science and Sanity: An Introduction to Non-Aristotelian Systems and General Semantics,* 3rd edition. International Non-Aristotelian Library Publishing Company, 1948.

Kropotkin, Petr. *Mutual Aid.* Boston: Extending Horizon Books, 1955.

Langer, Susanne K. *An Introduction to Symbolic Logic.* New York: Dover Publications, 1953.

Langer, Susanne K. *Philosophy in a New Key.* New York: Penguin, 1948.

Lawrence, D. H. *Selected Poems.* New York: Penguin, 1950.

Lawrence, Merle. *Studies in Human Behavior.* Princeton: Princeton University Press, 1949.

Lee, Irving. *Language Habits in Human Affairs.* New York: Harper & Brothers, 1941.

Lewin, Kurt. *A Dynamic Theory of Personality.* New York: McGraw-Hill, 1935.

Lieber, H. & L. *The Education of T. C. Mits.* New York: Norton, 1942.

Lieber, H. & L. *Mits, Wits, and Logic.* New York: Norton, 1947.

McDonald, John. *Strategy in Poker, Business, and War.* New York: Norton, 1950.

Montague, Ashley. *On Being Human.* New York: Henry Schuman, 1951.

Murphy, Gardner. *Personality.* New York: Harper & Brothers, 1947.

Neurath, Otto, Carnap, Rudolf, and Morris, Charles (eds.). *International Encyclopedia of Unified Science,* vols. I and II. Chicago: University of Chicago Press, 1955.

Newton, Norman T. *An Approach to Design.* Cambridge: Addison-Wesley, 1951.

Oppenheimer, J. Robert. *The Open Mind.* New York: Simon and Schuster, 1955.

Oppenheimer, J. Robert. *Science and the Common Understanding.* New York: Simon and Schuster, 1953.

Perls, Frederick, Hefferline, Ralph F., Goodman, Paul. *Gestalt Therapy.* New York: Julian Press, 1951.

Polya, G. *Induction and Analogy in Mathematics.* Princeton: Princeton University Press, 1954.

Ruesch, Jurgen, and Bateson, Gregory. *Communication, The Social Matrix of Psychiatry.* New York: Norton, 1951.

Sawyer, W. W. *Mathematician's Delight.* Harmondsworth: Penguin Books, 1943.

Schrödinger, Erwin. *What Is Life?* London: Cambridge University Press, 1951.

Shank, Bradford. *Fragments.* Published by author, Los Angeles, 1952.

Sondel, Bess. *Everyday Speech.* New York: Permabooks, 1950.

Sorokin, Pitirim. *Altruistic Love.* Boston: The Beacon Press, 1950.

Sorokin, Pitirim (ed.). *Explorations in Altruistic Love and Behavior.* Boston: The Beacon Press, 1950.

Stanislavski, Constantin. *An Actor Prepares*. New York: Mac-Gregor, 1952.

Sullivan, Harry Stack. *The Psychiatric Interview*. New York: Norton, 1954.

Thompson, Laura. *Culture in Crisis*. New York: Harper & Brothers, 1950.

Thompson, Sylvanus F. *Calculus Made Easy*. New York: The Macmillan Company, 1951.

Untermeyer, Louis. *The Poetry and Prose of Walt Whitman*. New York: Simon and Schuster, 1949.

Walker, Kenneth. *Venture with Ideas*. London: Jonathan Cape, 1951.

Watts, Alan W. *The Wisdom of Insecurity*. New York: Pantheon, 1951.

Whyte, Lancelot Law. *The Next Development in Man*. London: Cresset Press, 1944.

Wiener, Norbert. *The Human Use of Human Beings*. New York: Doubleday, 1954.

Wild, John. *The Challenge of Existentialism*. Bloomington: Indiana University Press, 1955.

Wilson, Richard A. *The Miraculous Birth of Language*. New York: Philosophical Library, 1948.

Young, J. Z. *Doubt and Certainty in Science*. London: Oxford University Press, 1951.

Zipf, George Kingsley. *Human Behavior and the Principle of Least Effort*. Cambridge: Addison-Wesley Press, 1949.

Index